ON
THE CHURCHLANDS

William Hirstein
Elmhurst College

THOMSON
WADSWORTH

Australia • Canada • Mexico • Singapore • Spain • United Kingdom • United States

Durham County Council Cultural Services	
CO 1 60 93378 70	
Askews	
191.9	

COPYRIGHT © 2004 Wadsworth,
a division of Thomson Learning, Inc.
Thomson Learning™ is a trademark
used herein under license.

ALL RIGHTS RESERVED. No part of
this work covered by the copyright
hereon, may be reproduced or used in
any form or by any means—graphic,
electronic, or mechanical, including,
but not limited to, photocopying,
recording, taping, Web distribution,
information networks, or information
storage and retrieval systems—without
the written permission of the publisher.

Printed in Canada
1 2 3 4 5 6 7 07 06 05 04 03

Printer: Transcontinental-Louiseville

ISBN: 0-534-57627-3

For more information about our
products, contact us at:
**Thomson Learning Academic
Resource Center
1-800-423-0563**

For permission to use material from
this text, contact us by:
Phone: 1-800-730-2214
Fax: 1-800-731-2215
Web: www.thomsonrights.com

Asia
Thomson Learning
5 Shenton Way #01-01
UIC Building
Singapore 068808

Australia/New Zealand
Thomson Learning
102 Dodds Street
Southbank, Victoria 3006
Australia

Canada
Nelson
1120 Birchmount Road
Toronto, Ontario M1K 5G4
Canada

Europe/Middle East/South Africa
Thomson Learning
High Holborn House
50-51 Bedford Row
London WC1R 4LR
United Kingdom

Latin America
Thomson Learning
Seneca, 53
Colonia Polanco
11560 Mexico D.F.
Mexico

Spain/Portugal
Paraninfo Thomson Learning
Calle/Magallanes, 25
28015 Madrid, Spain

Contents

Preface

1. Folk Psychology
Introduction	1
What is Folk Psychology?	3
Is Folk Psychology a Theory?	6
Conclusion	13

2. Eliminativism
Introduction	17
What is Reduction?	19
Will Folk Psychology Be Eliminated?	23
Sentences and Concepts	30
Successor Theories to Folk Psychology	32
Conclusion	34

3. Neurophilosophy
Introduction	38
The Psychology of Philosophers	43
Two Conceptions of Philosophy	46
The Brain: A Guide for Philosophers	51
Scientism	55

4. Consciousness
Introduction	61
Response to Dennett on Filling In	63
Response to Searle on Computers and Consciousness	65
Response to Jackson on Qualia	71
Response to Nagel on Introspection	73
Response to the 'Quantum Consciousness' Theories	79
Prototype of a Neurobiological Theory of Consciousness	82
Conclusion: The Imaginable and the Unimaginable	86

Bibliography 92

Preface

Paul and Patricia Churchland are philosophers and cognitive scientists currently working at the University of California, San Diego. In books and articles written over the last twenty-five years, they have urged philosophers to open themselves up to the current revolution in brain science. Many recent discoveries, they argue, are relevant to age-old philosophical issues about the nature of mind and consciousness, about the causes behind our actions, and especially about our conception of ourselves. They have created a new sub-discipline within philosophy devoted to this research program, called "neurophilosophy."

The Churchlands have avidly done what they recommend. They have brought a huge and varied body of scientific information into their philosophical writings. One of their most important theses, known as "eliminativism," is that this research shows that scientific theories about the brain do not square well with our traditional commonsense beliefs about the mind, and that this will force wholesale changes in the ways we think about our mental lives. This popular conception of the mind, which we all employ daily when we use terms such as "believe," "think," "see," "plan," and dozens of others, has been called "folk psychology."

During the last thirty years, a sea-change has occurred in the attitude of mainstream science toward the topics of what exactly consciousness is and how the brain produces it. While consciousness was once regarded as either non-existent, unimportant, or impenetrable with any scientific technique, it is now not only acceptable to write about, but all the rage. This situation, in which scientists and philosophers find themselves working on the same problems, has helped to generate interest in the work of the Churchlands. They have provided a clear view of the important philosophical and scientific data relevant to questions about consciousness, something which is immensely valuable in that it enables both philosophers and scientists to see how their research programs connect.

In order to make their case for the relevance of science to philosophical issues, the Churchlands have been compelled to argue against a conception of philosophy according to which scientific findings, by definition, are not relevant to philosophical problems. According to this conception, widely held among traditional philosophers, philosophers seek a different type of knowledge from that which the scientist seeks—the philosopher seeks *a priori* knowledge, or knowledge which is attainable without experience of the world. The Churchlands argue, however, that this conception of philosophy does not correctly describe its history or its current practice. They also point out that a close look at the history of philosophy reveals that many of the greatest philosophers had one foot in science and one in what is today considered philosophy, and moved effortlessly between the two disciplines.

More broadly, the Churchlands argue that we should give scientific findings more weight in our views of the world and of ourselves, and against the idea that it is somehow "scientistic," "reductionistic," or even blasphemous to attempt to account for our mental lives scientifically. The Churchlands' future-directed attitude is rare among philosophers, who tend to be more interested in understanding the past—the history of philosophy. They are constantly looking ahead, sometimes quite far ahead, at how discoveries in the sciences might change our conceptions of ourselves, and initiating debate on whether these changes are good or bad.

This is an introductory essay on the Churchlands' philosophy; it combines exposition of their views with analysis and criticism. It is meant to be accessible to the newcomer, while still being of interest to the expert. I will speak as frequently of the Churchlands, plural, as I do of Patricia Churchland and Paul Churchland for a reason: They share a basic outlook having to do with informing philosophy with neuroscience. They also think alike on many of the crucial issues in the philosophy of mind and philosophy in general. At the same time, they have taken full advantage of productive differences in their thinking. They never automatically agree on any issue, and often the agreement one does see came only after years of discussion between them.

I would like to thank the following people who informed and influenced my thinking on these issues: William Brenner, Melinda Campbell, George Graham, Rick Grush, Brian Keeley, Dan Kolak, Sandra de Mello, Erik Myin, Thomas Natsoulas, Dan Primozic, V.S. Ramachandran, John Smythies, John Sutton, Ron Wiginton and Richard Wollheim. Special thanks to Paul and Patricia Churchland for answering large numbers of questions and offering comments on the manuscript.

1
Folk Psychology

> *The realization that all of human knowledge is speculative and provisional is a highly liberating insight. It is also well-founded. We have the repeated empirical lessons of our own intellectual history to press the point upon us.*
>
> Paul Churchland, "Evaluating Our Self-Conception," 1993

Introduction

James drove into town because he *wanted* to see his friend Joann and he *believed* that she would be there, at their favorite bar. When he got there and *saw* her sitting cozily in a booth with Ralph, he *felt* crushed, and walked outside, *dazed* and *confused*.

We give these sorts of explanations every day when asked why someone did something. Aside from requiring knowledge of what words like "want," "believe," "see," and "feel" mean, notice the large amount of background knowledge we use in order to understand this little story. We know what it feels like to have our plans fall apart, what it's like to feel rejected, what it's like inside a bar, what sorts of things people do in bars, and on and on. There is also a large body of even more basic knowledge we employ: That driving into town takes at least several minutes, not several seconds or several days, that one enters a bar by the door, that James, Joann, and Ralph are normal adult human beings, and so on.

We are quite skilled at giving and understanding these explanations, whether for our own actions, or for the actions of others, but we tend not to notice how skilled we are, because our minds bring all of this knowledge into play so effortlessly. Giving such explanations is part of an activity which pervades our lives and which we learn very early on in life, which has been called "folk psychology." Folk-psychological explanations usually contain words such as those italicized above, which seem to refer to mental states and processes going on inside the person, in his *mind*.

When brain science develops further in the future, will it vindicate this way of talking, by showing that people really do have brain states called beliefs and wants? Or will it show that this was merely a convenient way of speaking we had, and that the brain does not literally contain beliefs and desires, or thoughts, or hopes? The Churchlands became widely known, first in philosophical circles, then in the wider cognitive science community, by defending the view that mature brain science will show folk psychology to be largely false and radically mistaken, leading to the elimination of its use among both scientists and the public at large. They called this view "eliminative materialism," in order to make it clear that, while they still believe that our mental lives have a completely physical explanation, this explanation will ultimately not be posed in the language of folk psychology.

The Churchlands' idea was not that *all* folk psychological concepts will be eliminated, but that many of them might be, while others might fragment into more than one scientific concept, and still others might be combined with other concepts to form new concepts. As they put it:

> Some current categories may be largely correct, for example, "visual perception,"; some, for example, "memory," "attention," and "consciousness," appear to be subdividing, budding, and regrouping; and some may be replaced entirely by high-level categories that are more empirically adequate.[1]

The thesis of eliminativism also contains the claim that folk-psychology is itself a sort of theory, and hence can be corrected or eliminated in much the same way that theories in science have been throughout its history. Several other writers have objected, though, that folk psychology is not a theory, and that it has quite different functions from a scientific theory. In this chapter we will first examine the nature of folk psychology, then turn to the debate over whether it is a theory.

What is Folk Psychology?

We spend much of the day observing other people, trying to understand what exactly they are up to and what they will do in the future, especially if it might involve us. It only makes sense that we would have by now developed techniques for doing this, such as folk psychology. "Folk psychology," says Paul Churchland,

> denotes the prescientific, commonsense conceptual framework that all normally socialized humans deploy in order to comprehend, predict, explain, and manipulate the behavior of humans and the higher animals. This framework...embodies our baseline understanding of the cognitive, affective, and purposive nature of people. Considered as a whole, it constitutes our conception of what a person is.[2]

Concepts of mental states, which are a crucial part of this framework, include those related to perception, such as *see*, *hear*, *feel*, *smell*, *taste*, *touch*, *sense*, *perceive*, and *recognize*. After perception comes thought, captured by concepts such as *believe*, *think*, *decide*, *imagine*, *envision*, *remember*, *know*, *plan*, *desire*, *want*, *need*, and *wish*. Thought is often (some would say always) mixed with emotion, captured by such concepts as *love*, *hate*, *fear*, *embarrassment*, *joy*, *disgust*, and *anger*. From this chemistry emerges a product: intentional, voluntary action, deeds, captured by concepts such as *move*, *do*, *run*, *hit*, and the countless action verbs. Folk psychology honors the idea that these divisions, between perception, thought and emotion, and action, are rough. Some of its concepts lie across their borders—*intention*, for instance, spans the thought-action divide, while concepts such as *inspect*, and *discern* span the division between perception and thought, while *ruminate* spans the boundary between thought and emotion.

One of the primary ways we have for assessing our children's mastery of folk psychological concepts is seeing whether they have mastered the use of the folk psychological verbs which express them, such as "believe," "think," and "see." But, the human species no doubt possessed many of these concepts before we possessed language, a fact which should warn us against tying folk psychology too closely to its linguistic expression. The concept of seeing, for instance, is vital to tracking prey: one needs to make sure that the prey does not see you. Traditional analytic philosophy, however, has taken the linguistic aspect of folk psychology very seriously. Philosophers of language especially have noticed that our folk-psychological talk is quite systematic. What they call "attitude reports," or "attitude ascriptions" cover a large part of folk-psychological talk. Attitude reports have the following "normal form":

[Subject term] [psychological verb] [object term].

The subject term is always a noun phrase of some sort: "I," "the President," "Dr. Michael DeBakey." Sometimes the object term is also another noun phrase, as in:

I see the President.

But also, the object term can be an entire sentence, as in:

James believes that the Earth is overpopulated.

One of the interesting subtleties involved in understanding sentences with psychological verbs in them is called *opacity*. Suppose Larry is driving to work in the morning. It's Monday, he doesn't feel much like going to work, and he is running late. So he is speeding sullenly along when suddenly a large car in the adjoining lane going about half his speed lurches in front of him. He brakes hard, swerves around the big car, and just as he goes by, gives the finger to what he can only discern is a male driver. When he gets to work, Larry is called into the boss's office, and promptly fired—alas, it was his boss he gave the finger to. The boss recognized Larry, but Larry failed to recognize his boss. Now, how do we describe to our co-workers who want to know why Larry is packing up his things what Larry did? Do we say, "On the way to work, Larry gave the finger to the boss?" The problem, of course, with saying this is that someone might think we mean that he gave his boss the finger *intentionally, knowingly, on purpose*, etc. Folk psychology uses concepts of this sort to patch up a curious hole in its explanatory framework, or at least its linguistic expression. What all this shows, however, is something rather amazing: We are sensitive not only to *what* particular things in the world a person is thinking about, but to the *way* in which the person thinks about them. So, in Larry's case for instance, we disallow the following inference:

(1) Larry saw a man in traffic this morning.

(2) That man was Larry's boss.

Therefore,

(3) Larry saw his boss in traffic this morning.

    The object term in (1), "a man" is called "opaque," because we are not allowed to substitute for it terms such as "his boss," even though they refer to the same person. This sensitivity to the way in which people represent the world gives folk psychology much greater accuracy in describing, explaining, and especially predicting behavior. In this case, if we learned that Larry *did* represent the man as his boss, we are much more surprised at his act. This would lead us to propose quite different explanations of his behavior, and to make different predictions about what he will do next.

    We are also selective about who exactly we apply folk psychology to. We only attribute beliefs to someone when we believe that she possesses the concepts necessary to form those beliefs. We might imagine a scientist, for example, who teaches his two-year old to say "$E = mc^2$." We would not say that the child has the belief expressed by this sentence, because we do not believe that he has concepts of energy, mass, and light. One folk-psychological test for concept acquisition is whether the person can properly identify the object or property that the concept represents. For instance, I will not allow that you have a concept of what a brake caliper is, if you cannot show me which thing on the brake assembly is the caliper, or you constantly call things calipers that are not calipers. Similarly, for our concepts which are responsible for representing particular things, a person needs to be able to re-identify that thing on different occasions before we allow that her concept is in order. If you call both George W. Bush and his brother Jeb Bush "the President," I will insist that you do not yet have a concept of the current president.

    Once acquired, concepts are promiscuous. Any concept can be combined with a given (usually quite large) subset of the person's other concepts to form beliefs or other thoughts. On the folk picture, beliefs and other states are complexes of concepts.[3] When you believe that Einstein was a scientist, and that Einstein worked in a patent office, our folk-psychological understanding of this is that the same concept participates in both beliefs. And this explains how you know (or really, why you assume) that both beliefs are about the same individual. The folk-psychological conception of beliefs then, seems to be that they consist of connections among a person's concepts. Your belief that Einstein was a scientist, for instance, consists of your concept of Einstein, connected to your concept of scientists. Concepts are the alphabet in which beliefs and other mental states, such as desires, memories, and so on, are spelled out.

Much remains to be clarified about the scope and nature of folk psychology, however. One ever-present danger in this discussion is mistaking the rather stiff, heavily language- and logic-based version of folk psychology of the analytic philosophers with the real thing in all its complexity. The role of emotions in our thinking and action, for instance, is largely neglected by these accounts. Similarly, the way in which our emotions interact with the emotions of others is also a very complex, but vital part of folk psychology. Is it part of folk psychology, for example, that we feel the instinctive need to hug someone when he or she begins crying? There are, in addition, other sorts of psychological activities we engage in which seem to fall midway between folk psychology and conventional scientific psychology. Is it part of folk psychology that we tend to think we can judge a person's character by the way he or she looks? There are also interesting questions about gender-based phenomena. Do men, for instance, apply different folk psychological theories to women than those they apply to other men? We need to formulate good answers to these and many other questions before we truly understand folk psychology.

Is Folk Psychology a Theory?

The philosopher of science Wilfred Sellars (1912-1989) was the first to broach the idea that folk psychology is a theory. In his essay "Empiricism and the Philosophy of Mind" (1956),[4] Sellars imagines a time in human history when people possess language, but do not have anything like folk psychology, so that there are no folk-psychological verbs in their language. But then a scientist, Jones, postulates the existence of what he calls "thoughts," which are mental events rather like covertly saying a sentence to oneself. Jones also postulates that people have sensations, which are internal versions of external objects (e.g., my visual sensation of a rose). However fanciful, the idea that folk psychology was at one point a sort of scientific breakthrough, or at least can be coherently treated as such, encourages the notion that it really is an early scientific theory. Paul Churchland claims that there are several properties common to scientific theories which folk psychology and the other folk theories possess:

> The term "folk psychology" is also intended to portray a parallel with what might be called "folk physics," "folk chemistry," "folk biology," and so forth. The term involves the deliberate implication that there is something *theory*-like about our commonsense understanding in all of these domains. The implication is that our relevant framework is speculative, systematic, and corrigible, that it embodies generalized information, and that it permits explanation and prediction in the fashion of any theoretical framework.[5]

One argument offered early on for the claim that folk psychology is a theory was that one could survey our folk-psychological behavior, such as the reporting of attitudes, and recover a number of claims which have the rough appearance of scientific laws, such as:

People who suffer bodily damage generally feel pain.

People who are angry are generally impatient.

People who fear that a certain event will happen generally hope that event will not happen.

People who desire something, and believe that a certain action will bring that thing about, and have no other preferred actions will generally engage in that action.[6]

We allow that each of these can be corrected via *ceteris paribus* clauses, which is why they make claims about what "generally happens." *Ceteris paribus* means "other things being equal," so the full version of one of the above, for example, would be, "Other things being equal, people who are angry are generally impatient." For instance, we allow that a parent might feel anger when dealing with a misbehaving child, but not let that anger give rise to impatience.

This is a rather wide notion of theory, however, which threatens to open the door for all sorts of things to count as theories, but the Churchlands are not deterred by this. Responding to a criticism by Kathleen Wilkes, Patricia Churchland outlines her broad conception of what counts as a theory:

> I see speculative theory implicit in practically every concept

we use; she finds theory only in professional scientific journals, and in the esoteric working-hours conversations of people in white lab coats. I see the mind-brain as being a furious and inveterate theory-maker and theory-user.... I see folk physics, folk thermodynamics, folk astronomy, folk topology, folk chemistry, folk sociology, folk economics, folk semantics, and sundry other folk theories peering out from almost every sentence we utter.[7]

Scientists distinguish theories from hypotheses by saving the word "theory" for a structured set of claims which has generated a wide body of confirmatory evidence. And indeed, the Churchlands' wide use of "theory" has not violated these criteria. The tenets of folk psychology do seem closer to theories than hypotheses, especially because of the way that "hypothesis" denotes something tentative, something under consideration. The claim that people generally feel pain when they suffer bodily damage, for instance, is not anything tentative, or under consideration, in our minds when we use folk psychology. We assume it, although there is still a difference between an assumption such as this, and the way that an evolutionary biologist would assume that the theory of evolution is true. For one thing, we were never explicitly taught that bodily damage causes pain.

But what if our ability to learn and employ folk psychology is innate, or what if there are brain areas devoted to accomplishing folk psychology that are not used when normal scientific theories are employed? Either of these possibilities tends to work against the Churchlands' idea that our brains embody and employ folk psychology in the same way they might a scientific theory, although neither decisively rules that out. The idea that folk psychology qualifies as a scientific theory, albeit a very old one, has become more controversial as we have begun to learn more about how humans understand the actions of other humans. If the ability to use folk psychology is either innate or employs special brain structures or processes, this may also mean that we cannot abandon it the way we abandoned Ptolemy's theory of the cosmos as earth-centered. Minimally, it seems to imply that the way we think about ourselves and other people might be radically different from the way we think about objects. But "we must resist the temptation," says Paul Churchland, "to see in these questions a renewed motivation for counting folk psychology as special...."[8]

How exactly do humans understand the actions of other humans? According to one approach, I understand your intentional behavior by employing a *simulation* of your mind; I create a model of your mind, inside my mind. If I assume that your mind is similar to my mind, I can use my knowledge of my own mind to understand you. From its early beginnings in William Dilthey's concept of *verstehen*, to more recent work by Donald Davidson,[9] Alvin Goldman,[10] and Robert Gordon[11] on the subject of *mental simulation*, philosophers have tried to discern how we understand each other so easily and naturally. Simulation theorists have explicitly challenged the Churchlands' theory-oriented approach, by arguing that simulating is quite different from applying a theory. Simulating is usually done more automatically and less intentionally than applying a theory, they argue. It also is more a sort of knowing *how* than knowing *that*. We know *how* to speak a language, for instance, but we have very little conception of the actual grammatical rules which govern our language use. The Churchlands' view that folk psychology is a theory is lent support, though, by the recent trend toward describing this modeling activity as involving the possession of a *theory of mind*.[12]

One objection which the Churchlands have made to the simulation theory is that knowledge about our own minds may come *after* the learning of the theory of folk psychology, rather than coming first, as on the simulation theory:

> The capacity for knowledge of one's own mind may already presuppose the general knowledge that [folk psychology] embodies.[13]

Certainly there is truth to this; folk psychology provides a framework for thinking about the mind, and its myriad concepts greatly increase the range of thoughts we can form about our own minds. But again, the Churchlands seem to have a more explicit sort of knowledge in mind. The adaptation of mental processes which normally represent me to the purpose of representing you can happen at more reflexive, less intentional levels. Think of the way we automatically flinch when we see someone struck, for instance.

It is interesting to notice that on the simulation view of folk psychology, if I am using my mind as a model or theory, the assumption is that I am using my actual mind, with its actual properties, so that by its very nature, simulation theory contains a tacit assumption that folk psychology is correct. But another objection Paul Churchland has given is to argue that the conception of human nature contained in folk psychology goes far beyond our conceptions of ourselves in particular:

> A generalization from one's own case may be…explanatorily

too narrow in its scope to account for the full range and robustness of one's general knowledge of human nature....[14]

This seems right, but at least part of this additional knowledge may also be capturable by a simulation theory. During the course of our lives, we become aware of a set of distinct character types. A strong-willed character type, for instance, energetic and hard-driving, assertive and unself-conscious. We make different sorts of predictions about what a person of this sort might do when confronted with an obstacle, for instance. Our knowledge of these types is partly simulatory, we understand what it would be like to be someone with that type of character. We often fit people we meet into one of these types in order to better understand them, although we are also often mistaken when we apply this typology. As we get older and wiser, we add to this repertoire of character types, so that we can apply them to more people, and make more accurate predictions about what they might do.

One of the hoped-for benefits of developing theories about how people accomplish folk psychology is that it might shed some light on the mystery of autism. Autism is a developmental disorder marked by a delay in learning language, a tendency to engage in simple, repetitive behaviors, and most importantly, a lack of interest in other people. Autistic people are relevant here because they can possess many of the normal cognitive abilities, while lacking the ability to use folk psychology. If autistic people are not good at employing folk psychology, but good at applying other folk theories, this may be evidence in favor of the idea that we use special brain processes to exercise our abilities at folk psychology. There is in fact some recent evidence that a part of the problem in autism is that autistic people *do* use the same brain areas to perceive and think about both people and objects, unlike normal people, who use different brain areas. Researchers who observed brain activity (via functional magnetic resonance imaging) of autistic people identifying faces found activity in their brains "consistent with feature-based strategies that are more typical of nonface recognition."[15]

Research relating autism to the question of what special processes we bring to the perception of others has focused on the cognitive aspect of the difficulty autistic people have in understanding others. So, for instance, a large amount of literature has been directed at the apparent inability of autistic children to attribute false beliefs to other people.[16] In a typical false belief task, the child is shown a puppet playing with a toy. The puppet puts the toy in a box, then leaves the area. While the first puppet is gone, a second puppet enters, takes the toy out of the box and hides it in a cupboard. Then the first puppet returns, and the child is asked where the puppet will look for his toy. The task requires the child to distinguish where the toy *actually* is from where the puppet *believes* the toy is. At around age four, normal children have developed the ability to answer correctly, that the puppet will look in the box, because that is where he believes the toy is; before that age, they tend to point to the cupboard. Autistic children ages four and well beyond still tend to point to the cupboard, presumably because they lack the ability to see the situation from the point of view of the first puppet.

One of the ways in which the brain appears hardwired to perform simulations is by its employment of *mirror neurons*. Mirror neurons are active either when *I* do x, or I see *you* do x.[17] Hence they receive input from both the visual system and the somatosensory system. They were discovered accidentally when researchers were recording activity in monkeys from a part of the brain thought to be solely a fine motor control area for the arm and hand. These cells fired either when the monkey picked up an object or—to the researchers' great surprise—when the monkey simply *saw* one of the researchers pick up the object. Apparently, the monkey's brain uses its motor areas to understand the actions of others. Again, this gives the appearance that folk psychology employs special brain areas or processes and hence that the brain treats it differently from the way it treats knowledge of scientific theories.

One sort of response the Churchlands could make to this would be to argue that the existence of mirror neurons merely shows that our understanding of others will be based on our understanding of ourselves, *whatever that understanding is*. Folk psychology may be merely one of a variety of different simulation-based theories. There are two other lines of response the Churchlands might give to the idea that the practice of folk psychology employs special-purpose cognitive structures. One is to argue that the use of mirror neurons is a basic engineering solution to several different types of problem, and that they may be found at several levels of the nervous system and in several different brain systems, so that they are not unique to the higher brain processes which accomplish folk psychology. Another line of response would be to argue, as the philosopher Henri Bergson did in the early 1900s, that we do in fact have two ways of understanding, but that these two ways are applied to objects as well as people:

> We get to know a thing, Bergson says, either by circling around it, or by entering into it. If we stay outside, the result depends on our standpoint and is expressed in symbols

Folk Psychology

[Bergson called this "analysis"], whereas in the second kind of cognition we follow the life of the thing in an empathic identification with it [Bergson called this "intuition"].[18]

We apply intuition even to objects. For instance, if we see a piano fall out of a moving truck and smash on the pavement, we cannot help feeling a little squeamish, as if we are imagining what it might be like to experience that ourselves. If Bergson is correct, this shows that the abilities we use in folk psychology are not applied only to humans, but rather, generalize to all objects. The existence of *animism* among primitive peoples (in which trees, clouds, mountains, and so on are given human attributes) lends support to the idea: We naturally tend to apply intuition to everything, at least until we become convinced that doing so is simply not effective—or we fall under the sway of theory, the Churchlands might add.

The objections to viewing folk psychology as a scientific theory not only misconstrue folk-psychology, but science itself as well, according to the Churchlands. Paul Churchland argues that objections of this sort employ a conception of scientific theories which is too language-based. Their proponents observe that our knowledge of others does not consist of a set of propositions, but rather a model, and then mistakenly reason that hence it does not constitute a theory. Folk psychology is a theory, but learning it also involves learning much more than propositions, he argues. One is also learning a social practice, as is the case with any theory. Paul Churchland:

> Since Thomas Kuhn's 1962 book, *The Structure of Scientific Revolutions*, it has been evident that learning theories peculiar to any discipline is not solely or even primarily a matter of learning a set of laws and principles: it is a matter of learning a complex social practice, of entering a specialized community with shared values and expectations, both of the world and of each other.[19]

The strategy, then, is to move folk psychology and science closer together by portraying our understanding of folk psychology as more science-like than we thought, while portraying science as more folk-like than we thought. While no one denies that the practice of science has important social elements, these elements are different in quality from those involved in folk psychology, however. There is an important difference in function between traditional scientific theories and folk psychology, which shows itself strongly in the influence of social factors. One of the main functions of folk psychology is surely to synchronize and harmonize our behavior by regulating its explanation according to the same scheme of concepts. Thus, folk psychology works well when we all think alike. Given this, it may be that the wide applicability of folk psychology helps to explain the effectiveness that it does possess. Even if the simulation theory is correct, my use of myself to understand you only gives a special advantage over other general-purpose cognitive abilities if you are in fact similar to me. But, if you do not practice a folk psychology of the sort that I do, my folk psychology may not provide a good theory of you. Science, on the other hand, dies when scientists all think alike. Disagreement is the fuel which both moves science forward and keeps it honest: Theories are tested against one another, scientists strive to find flaws in the theories of their peers. Those outside of science frequently misunderstand this and think that disagreement among proponents of a particular research program signals its demise. It is exactly the opposite, those programs which are frozen, which force agreement among their scientists, are the ones in danger.

Conclusion

One might try a different approach to this problem by asking the following question: Does the fact that folk psychology was constructed by our brains make it more likely to be true of our brains? If folk psychology is a theory, its structure is determined, ideally, by two factors: First, it is determined by brain activity itself, in the same way that the theory of evolution is determined by the facts of inheritance, selection and so on. But also, the structure and content of folk psychology is constrained by our brain's proclivities. Both of these claims are true of all theories; however, the degree of constraint may be especially great in the case of folk psychology.

Another point worth noting concerns Sellars' original description of folk psychology. One criticism of Sellars' thought experiment is that there is not enough detail in his story to cover the complexity and subtlety of folk psychology. The protoscientist Jones takes the overt declarative sentences current in his society as his model, but all attempts to understand folk-psychological ascriptions on the model of overt declarative sentences have failed, primarily because they could not account for the phenomenon of opacity. Our ascriptions somehow manage to combine an overt declarative sentence with a claim about covert mental representations, at least on some current theories of how to attach truth values to them.

According to Mark Crimmens' and John Perry's account of belief ascriptions, they serve a dual purpose of referring both to their normal external referents and to the mental representations which the target person has of those referents.[20] So, in the case of Larry above, the reason why we balk at agreeing to the sentence "Larry saw his boss in traffic," is that the term "his boss" does indeed refer to the right man (the external referent), but it also refers to Larry's concept of his boss. We balk at the sentence because *that concept* was not involved in his act of seeing, so the words "his boss" ("tacitly") refer to the wrong concept. This allows Crimmens and Perry to assign the correct truth values to the sorts of ascriptions we examined above, where someone fails to properly represent certain objects, and hence their theory can explain opacity. There is an obvious connection between theories such as this and the simulation theory: Tacit reference is accomplished by the model of the person's mind. For example, in the case of Jack, we create a concept of Jack's boss in our minds in order to model Jack's mind, and that very concept is the one which tacitly refers to Jack's concept of his boss.

It is too early to tell exactly which ways folk psychology is and is not similar to typical scientific theories. But we will learn more about this relatively soon as science uncovers more about autism, and the brain in general. In the next chapter, we will move to the question of whether folk psychology, whatever its nature, will be eliminated when scientists finally discover the principles behind the working of the brain.

Endnotes

[1] Patricia Churchland and V.S. Ramachandran, "Filling In: Why Dennett is Wrong," in *On the Contrary: Critical Essays, 1987-1997*, Paul M. Churchland and Patricia S. Churchland, Cambridge, Mass.: The MIT Press, 1998.

[2] Paul Churchland, "Folk Psychology," in *On the Contrary: Critical Essays, 1987-1997*, Paul M. Churchland and Patricia S. Churchland, Cambridge, Mass.: The MIT Press, 1998.

[3] See Stephen Stich, *From Folk Psychology to Cognitive Science*, Cambridge, Mass.: The MIT Press, 1983, 78.

[4] In Vol. 1 of *Minnesota Studies in the Philosophy of Science*, eds. H. Feigl and M. Scriven, Minneapolis: The University of Minnesota Press. Also published in Sellars' book *Science, Perception, and Reality*, London: Routledge and Kegan Paul, 1963.

[5] "Folk Psychology," 4.

[6] *Ibid.*, 6.

[7] "Replies to Comments," [Symposium on *Neurophilosophy*] *Inquiry* **29** (1987), 247-248.

[8] *A Neurocomputational Perspective: The Nature of Mind and the Structure of Science* (1989), Cambridge, Mass.: The MIT Press, 122.

[9] Donald Davidson, "On Saying That," *Synthese* **19** (1968-1969), 130-146.

[10] Alvin I. Goldman, "Interpretation Psychologized," *Mind and Language* **4** (1989), 161-185.

[11] Robert Gordon, *The Structure of Emotions: Investigations in Cognitive Philosophy*, New York: Cambridge University Press, 1987.

[12] See for instance the essays in *Understanding Other Minds*, eds. Simon Baron-Cohen, Helen Tager-Flugsberg, and Donald J. Cohen, Oxford: Oxford Univ. Press, 2000.

[13] See "Folk Psychology," 12.

[14] *Ibid*.

[15] See "Abnormal Ventral Temporal Cortical Activity During Face Discrimination Among Individuals with Autism and Asperger Syndrome," by Robert T. Schultz, *et al.*, *Archives of General Psychiatry* **57** (2000), 331-340.

Also see "Autonomic Responses of Autistic Children to People and Objects," by William Hirstein, Portia Iversen, and V.S. Ramachandran, *Proceedings of the Royal Society of London, Series B: Biological Sciences* **268** (2001), 1883-1888. We found that, unlike normal people, autistic children have the same autonomic responses to people and objects.

[16] See "Does the Autistic Child Have a Theory of Mind?," by Simon Baron-Cohen, Alan M. Leslie, and Uta Frith, *Cognition* **21** (1983), 37-46; see also "Beliefs About Beliefs: Representation and Constraining

Function of Wrong Beliefs in Young Children's Understanding of Deception," by H. Wimmer and J. Perner, *Cognition* **13** (1983), 103-128.

[17] See the work of Giacomo Rizzolatti, including V. Gallese, L. Fadiga, L. Fogassi, and G. Rizzolatti, "Action Recognition in the Premotor Cortex," *Brain* **119** (1996), 592-609; and G. Rizzolatti, L. Fadiga, V. Gallese, and L. Fogassi, "Premotor Cortex and the Recognition of Motor Actions," *Cognitive Brain Research* **3(2)** (1996), 131-141.

[18] From *Bergson*, by Leszek Kolakowski, Oxford: Oxford Univ. Press, 1985, 24.

[19] *On the Contrary: Critical Essays 1987-1997*, Cambridge, Mass.: The MIT Press, 1998, 11.

[20] See *Talk About Beliefs*, by Mark Crimmens, Cambridge, Mass.: The MIT Press, 1992.

2
Eliminativism

> *The adequacy of folk psychology is in no way secured by its seeming to be overwhelmingly obvious, by its being observationally applied, by its being applied introspectively, or even by its being innate, if such is the case.*
>
> Patricia Churchland
> *Neurophilosophy*, 1986

Introduction

The philosopher leaves our everyday world, dives down several levels and, at the crucial place, sees exactly how the brain generates our mental lives. But when she returns to the surface, she finds herself not at the familiar folk-psychological level from which she left, but in an entirely new and strange place. The Churchlands did not begin their study of neuroscience with the intention of unseating folk psychology, but rather, found that when they began learning about the brain they simply could not fit what they learned into the traditional view. This led them to suggest that much of folk psychology would be eliminated in the coming years as we begin to develop more powerful theories of brain structure and function. They were the first to envision what a psychology which *is* well grounded in the way the brain actually works might be like. Their vision was that it would be quite different from folk psychology.

The Churchlands had doubts at the outset about whether the rather strong term "eliminativism" properly captured the selectivity of their view:

> In 1986, I [Patricia Churchland] agreed with Keith Campbell that some term other than "eliminative materialism" would be preferable. (The expression was originally coined by an avowed opponent of the position, Richard Cornman.) [Paul Churchland] and I stewed quite a lot about this word when he was writing his book *Matter and Consciousness* (1984) and I was writing *Neurophilosophy* (1986). We thought that "revisionary materialism" was closer to what we wanted to convey, inasmuch as we take it to be an empirical question how much revision a theory and its concepts will undergo, where outright elimination occupies but one end of a wide spectrum.[1]

The idea that folk psychology, or large parts of it, might be eliminated occurred to Paul Churchland during the writing of his dissertation as the product of a set of claims, each of which seemed to him to be independently plausible.[2] Once one sees that all of our other folk theories (folk physics, folk chemistry, etc.) have been replaced by modern scientific theories; and one sees that the theory replaced is shown to be false; and, further, one sees that folk psychology is in fact a theory, the idea that folk psychology may well be replaced and found to be false follows inductively. One reason perhaps why this hadn't been noticed before is that no one had noticed, until Paul Churchland's teacher Wilfred Sellars did, that folk psychology is importantly theory-like.

Strongly worded objections immediately arose, however, when Paul Churchland went public with the view in 1979 in his first book, *Scientific Realism and the Plasticity of Mind*.[3] First, went one objection, isn't it simply foolhardy to deny something that we confirm the correctness of several times a day? Folk psychology works smoothly most of the time, doesn't it? At the very least, we often find that folk-psychological explanations satisfy our curiosity. But the apparent obviousness of folk psychology is, says Patricia Churchland, "a familiarity phenomenon, rather than a measure of metaphysical truth."[4] Apparent obviousness alone is no argument for truth. It seems obvious that the sun moves around the earth, or at least it did for thousands of years, before astronomy showed that this piece of folk astronomy is an illusion.

There were also objections which had an ethical basis. The

objections were primarily to the effect that what was getting eliminated was more than just a way of speaking about ourselves; the elimination of folk psychology threatens to rip the heart out of the conception of ourselves required for civilized society, cried the dissenters. Our conception of intentional as opposed to unintentional action, for instance, and the associated notion of responsibility for actions and events, so vital in any legal case, is central to the way we run our society. Hence, Richard Swinburne said that the eliminativist view, is "a salutary warning to all who would too readily abandon the dualistic insights of their forefathers."[5] And, "it is morally abhorrent," decreed R.A. Sharpe, "to suggest that neurological information is any alternative to a deeper sympathetic understanding of persons."[6]

In response, the Churchlands have taken care to explain that a switch to a scientifically grounded theory bodes well rather than ill for our conceptions of ourselves. They agree that folk psychology embodies the ways we think about each other, and that this includes our moral and emotional conceptions of each other, but they argue that this does not imply we should preserve it at all costs. The good changes which come in these conceptions will outweigh the bad, according to the Churchlands. Patricia Churchland points out how "the 'biologizing' of such mental complaints as chronic depression and obsessive compulsive disorder, and their treatment with serotonin enhancers like Prozac, for example, have brought enormous relief to many sufferers."[7] Even if there were good ethical objections against elimination, those are not, one suspects, enough to keep it from happening, if we really came to believe that folk psychology is false and that its terms fail to refer to events in the brain.

What is Reduction?

Many of the arguments for eliminativism and their replies are posed in terms of a *reduction* of a higher-level theory to a lower-level one: The Churchlands claim that one way we will see that folk psychology is false is that we will find we are unable to successfully reduce it to neurobiology. The initial question about reduction in general concerns what exactly is being reduced, the theories, or the things the theories are about? That is, are we speaking of an *epistemic* reduction of one theory to another, or an *ontological* reduction of one type of thing or set of phenomena to another? There is another basic distinction between eliminative reduction, in which the higher-level phenomena simply disappear, and non-eliminative reduction, in which the higher-level phenomena are thought to still exist. Thus, the notion of reduction, according to Patricia Churchland,

> does not entail that the reduced theory will somehow cease to be, or that the phenomena it describes cease to be. On the contrary, if the reduction is smooth, its reduction gives it—and its phenomena—a firmer place in the larger scheme of biological theory.[8]

The thesis of eliminativism does of course include the idea that folk psychology will cease to be. But the Churchlands are clear that there will be some sort of replacement theory working at the same level at which folk psychology functioned. This new theory will have a firm place in biological theory, because it will be based on actual neurobiology. The theory will non-eliminatively reduce to biology.

The Churchlands prefer to think of reduction as a relation between theories; a reduced theory stands in a certain relation to a more basic theory. Claims that one phenomenon reduces to another phenomenon "are derivative upon the more basic claim that the theory that characterizes the first reduces to the theory that characterizes the second."[9] Patricia Churchland says that, "by making theories the fundamental relata, much of the metaphysical bewilderment and dottiness concerning how entities or properties could be reduced simply vanished."[10] Hence the question of whether mental states are reducible to brain states

> must be posed first in terms of whether some theory concerning the nature of mental states is reducible to a theory describing how neuronal ensembles work, and second whether it reduces in such a way that the mental states of T_R [the theory being reduced] can be identified with the neuronal states of T_B [the more basic theory].[11]

Reduction very often does not preserve the meanings of the reduced terms, however: "Light," for instance, does not mean the same thing as "electromagnetic radiation." A single term in the reduced theory might also be reduced to several terms in the reducing theory, or vice-versa.[12]

The mind-body problem is an ancient philosophical problem concerning how our minds relate to our bodies. In our context, the question is whether our theory of the mind can reduce, eliminatively or not, to our theories about physical objects. Nowadays, since we are quite sure that the part of our bodies most intimately related to our

Eliminativism

minds are our brains, it might more appropriately be called the mind-brain problem. The candidate solutions to this problem fall into two main categories: Dualism, the view that our minds consist either of some non-physical substance or set of properties, and materialism, the view that the mind is physical. The reason why the mind-body problem *is* ancient is that our minds, for some curious reason which has never been properly elucidated, do not seem to be physical, and this has given dualism a strong intuitive appeal. For instance, unlike other physical things, objects in the mind seem to disappear (or, even more curiously, to slowly fade away) when we cease attending to them. Dualism has always been the predominant view among the general public, but the majority of scientists and philosophers working on the problem are materialists. The longstanding task for them has been to explain how something physical such as the brain is capable of producing the amazing phenomena we associate with our minds.

The mind-body problem can be understood as a problem about the reduction of folk psychology to brain science, according to Paul Churchland:

> A ... consequence [of the idea that folk psychology is a theory] is that the traditional mind-body problem emerges as a straightforward scientific question—as a question of how the theoretical framework of [folk psychology] will turn out to be related to whatever neuropsychological theory might emerge to replace it.[13]

Thus the different positions on the mind-body problem correspond to positions about the reduction of folk psychology:

> If [folk psychology] reduces smoothly to a materialist successor theory, then the identity theory will be vindicated. If it proves disjunctively so "reducible," then functionalism will be vindicated. If it proves irreducible by reason of finding no adequate materialist successor at all, then some form of dualism will be vindicated. And if it proves irreducible by reason of failing utterly to map onto its successful materialist successor theory, then a position called eliminative materialism will be vindicated.[14]

The idea of reduction implies that our theories (and perhaps also the phenomena they describe) come in levels. Biology occupies a level above that of chemistry, which occupies a level above physics, and so on. The study of the brain involves several such levels, which can be described roughly by the order of magnitude of the sizes of the objects of interest at that level, or of the distances between the objects:

[1 Meter]:	Central Nervous System
[10 Centimeters]:	Brain Systems
[1 Centimeter]:	Topographic Maps
[1 Millimeter]:	Circuits
[100 Microns]:	Neurons
[1 Micron]:	Synapses
[10 Angstroms]:	Molecules

Figure 2.1: *Levels of organization in the nervous system.*

The levels can also be understood as functional levels, an approach which is not inconsistent with understanding them spatially. A functional understanding of the levels is allied with a way of thinking about causal relations as happening within a certain level, and not (usually) happening between objects at different levels. We do not, for instance, talk about how the carburetor in a car interacts with a molecule in the engine block. This would be an inappropriate mix of engineering and chemistry. Rather, we speak about the carburetor interacting with other objects existing at its level, such as the fuel pump, or the intake manifold. Very often the sorts of causal relations one sees at one level are entirely absent at other levels.

Phenomena at a lower level require some sort of amplification process before their effects appear at the next level up. Cancer, for instance, begins at a micro level with changes in the cell. Its amplification procedure is simply to increase the number of cells which are cancerous, or "immortal" because they do not die like regular cells, i.e., it produces tumors. When the cells become great enough in number, they can make their effects emerge at the macro level, by blocking some vital bodily function, such as digestion, circulation, or respiration.

One of the primary tasks of cognitive scientists is to understand exactly which levels are the crucial ones for their phenomena of interest, such as perception, action, and thought. The default strategy here is to start at the top level and descend until one finds the place where the linchpins and pivot points—the "guts" as it were—of the phenomena reside. This is typically also the level at which the phenomena can be most easily manipulated. The question of the ontological status of these levels is indeed a vexing problem of metaphysics and the philosophy of science. Philosophers of mind attempting to solve the mind-body problem earnestly hope that they can just assume the existence of these levels and focus on other aspects of the problem. But the sobering possibility remains that solving the mind-brain problem might require a better understanding of the nature of these levels and their interactions.

Will Folk Psychology Be Eliminated?

It is important to be clear that the Churchlands do not merely believe that folk psychology is old-fashioned or vague. They believe that as a whole it is demonstrably false in several respects:

> *Our commonsense psychological framework is a false and radically misleading conception of the causes of human behavior and the nature of cognitive activity.* On this view, folk psychology is not just an incomplete representation of our inner natures; it is an outright *mis*representation of our internal states and activities.[15]

On the other side are a diverse collection of *folk-psychological realists*,[16] who believe that folk-psychological explanations are frequently true, and that their constituent terms, such as "believe," and "remember," do refer to real brain states and processes. It is important to connect folk psychology to brain science, on a realist conception, because then we will have a science of the mind that is immediately useful and widely and easily applicable. It would also not only save our current conception of ourselves, but place it on a firmer footing. One type of realist argues for the reality of folk psychology as a true description of what we might think of as the software of the brain.[17] Our brains operate on proposition-sized data structures just as computers operate on their data, they suggest. There can also be interesting and useful descriptions of these operations which do not mention biological features of the brain, on this conception. These realists are the doctrinal descendents of the logical behaviorists and the classical theorists in artificial intelligence.

There are also realists who believe as strongly as the Churchlands in the direct relevance of neuroscience to philosophical questions about the mind, but who see in the brain confirmations of the hypotheses of folk psychology rather than refutations. It would be odd, they reason, if something as complex and intricate as folk psychology did not sink more deeply into the brain than the Churchlands allow. On the Churchlands' view, all of the signs and symptoms we have of folk psychology, all of the language and outward behaviors, all of the introspectively observable phenomena, are like a computer's user interface, which hides a completely different architecture and set of principles according to which it operates, a phenomenon known as the *user illusion*. But even in the case of the computer, there is a significant portion of the account of how the computer works which is devoted to describing this top-level interface. Folk psychology may not sink deeply into the brain, but at a minimum it describes a significant level of brain function, associated with consciousness. This level may be unique to humans and a few other higher primates, and may be the feature that makes us different and so much more cognitively effective than the other animals, or so the folk-psychological realist reasons.

One of the Churchlands' most frequent criticisms of the realists is that they put too much trust in the deliverances of introspection, which frequently seem to confirm folk psychology. But, they argue, the brain's real principles of operation are particularly opaque to introspection. Patricia Churchland says that

> Introspection reveals almost nothing about how nervous systems work, and from an evolutionary perspective, there is no reason why it should.[18]

In her view, this leads to a catalog of errors which introspection makes us prone to:

> If anything, human brains have a positive tendency to be misled about their nature. They tend to suppose they are not part of the biological order, that they are the result of special creation, that nervous tissue itself is not relevant to the understanding of the mind, and that introspection yields incontrovertible truths about a nonphysical mind, about the nature of free will, experience, knowledge, meaning, and

language. What the evolutionary and neurobiological perspective makes evident, however, is that to understand how the brain works, introspection is unreliable.[19]

But the Churchlands do not offer a reason for why our tendency to be misled exists. Nor do they discuss whether it exists for a reason at all, i.e., whether it may simply be an accident of evolution. In computer science, for instance, there is a reason for the user illusion: Since knowledge of the machine's actual workings is not important for the user, an interface is set up in order to present information in a form the user finds easy to understand. But of course, this sort of option is not open to the Churchlands as an explanation for the brain's massive deception, since computers are man-made artifacts, built with a specific purpose and plan, and human beings are not. Another interesting question the charges of illusion suggest is, who is getting misled? Since the Churchlands presumably believe that the folk-psychological sense of self is produced by the brain, this means that some part of the brain is misleading some other part of the brain—rather curious, and again, one is led to ask why?

Let us turn to some of the specific arguments for the idea that folk psychology will eventually disappear, and consider responses which realists about folk psychology either have given or might give:

Folk Beliefs Are Notoriously Wrong

If one looks at our history of thought about the universe, much of what we have believed throughout history is in fact not the case. The earth is not flat, as it appears, but spherical. The sun does not rise and set, we rotate daily on an axis. Similarly, nothing in our folk conception of ourselves prepared us for the idea that we evolved from non-living matter. Folks, in short, tend to get things wrong, at least in the early phases.

Science is also fallible though. The history of science is a history of our discoveries that our existing theories are not adequate, and need to be replaced with more correct, more comprehensive ones. Often the problem with a theory is traceable to belief in a non-existent substance. At one time, for instance, it was thought that the difference between a living organism and a recently expired one was that the living organism's body still contained a special fluid—which came to be known as *elan vital*, or vital spirit. But of course this substance was never found: Life is not a substance but a process. Similarly, scientists in the eighteenth and nineteenth centuries believed that heat is a fluid held in certain things, which they called "caloric." The more caloric a thing has, the hotter it is, the theory went. But no such fluid was ever found. Rather, scientists eventually realized that heat is simply molecular motion—the faster the molecules in a substance are moving, the hotter it is.[20]

The Churchlands suggest that folk concepts such as *belief* and *desire* will eventually suffer a similar fate. But there are crucial differences between concepts such as *vital spirit* and *caloric*, and concepts such as *belief*, a folk-psychological realist might object. Belief and desire are close us in a way that caloric is not. We have a kind of immediate access to our beliefs and desires that we do not have with caloric. We can actually experience our thoughts, beliefs, and desires, one might argue. As we have seen however, the Churchlands believe it is a mistake to take the products of introspection at face value. They would respond that we are indeed experiencing *something*, but it is not clear that that something is a belief or a thought. We might be mistaken in the same way as the people who believed that they could actually see witches in old Salem. They were seeing *someone*, but since witches do not really exist, they were not seeing *witches*. Their concept of witches did not successfully reduce to anything objective.

Folk Psychology is Too Limited in Scope

One reason why theories in science are replaced is that they fail to explain a wide enough range of phenomena, and a more comprehensive theory is developed. The behavior of children prior to their learning language, for instance, is not well captured by folk psychology, nor is the behavior of intelligent animals. We are all familiar with the charge that someone is speaking about her pet dog or cat anthropomorphically, for instance, by applying folk-psychological terms to it. Part of what we find mistaken about such behavior is that it seems like a misdescription: If a dog cannot believe that his master will take him for a walk next Wednesday (because he lacks the linguistic capacity to represent an event of that sort), should we then be saying apparently less objectionable things such as, "He believes his master is at the door"?

Folk psychology, according to the Churchlands, fails to explain "mental illness, sleep, creativity, memory, intelligence differences, and the many forms of learning."[21] This is a diverse list; while neuroscience has had some success explaining certain types of memory and learning, even it is still stymied by the mysteries of creativity, mental illness, and intelligence differences. But the real question for the future becomes whether folk psychology can smoothly expand to

Eliminativism

begin to account for these things, or whether we will find it better to start over with an entirely new sort of theory. Folk psychology may genuinely have a kind of shallowness, due to the fact that it operates at only the highest, conscious levels of the cognitive system, so that much of what happens in the levels beneath is unavailable to us. This is not, however, in itself evidence for its falsity or inadequacy at that higher level.

Folk Psychology Has Failed to Make Progress

Making progress is an important criterion for scientific theories to satisfy; progress and change are signs of a healthy scientific research program. Stagnation invites suspicion, and may indicate that the theory in question is not good science, or not science at all, an argument frequently used against creationists, whose main center, the Institute for Creation Research, had its institutional accreditation revoked because it was using textbooks more than one hundred years old.

Folk psychology, the Churchlands charge, has not progressed significantly in 2500 years. Contrary to this, it is sometimes argued that Sigmund Freud, for example, is responsible for certain additions to folk psychology: the idea of the unconscious motive, of the Oedipus complex, of the "Freudian slip," of dreams as disguised wishes, and so on. Even if these notions have become part of folk psychology, which is arguable, this tends not to help in its defense, since most of Freud's work is not considered scientific by the contemporary science community. Indeed, the case of Freud might be used against the folk-psychological realist: The Churchlands could argue that his failure to regiment folk psychology into science is exactly what they would have predicted.

Folk psychology has, however, changed over the years in terms of the sorts of entities it is applied to. At one time people applied it to objects such as mountains, clouds and trees—a practice known as *animism*. But on the whole, it is clear that folk psychology is not progressing in the way that contemporary scientific theories are. Again though, this can play into the hands of the person who argues that folk psychology is not a theory, but rather a means of regulating and coordinating our behaviors.

The Closure Problem

One problem inherent in folk psychology, or at least on one conception of it, is known as the closure problem: Are believers tacitly committed to all of the logical consequences of their beliefs? That is, if a person believes that p, and p implies q, does this imply that the person also believes that q? Those philosophers employing a heavily logic- and language-based conception of folk psychology ran into this problem. But, contrary to the idea that we are committed to believing everything our beliefs imply, we very often think of someone as not being particularly good at following out the logical consequences of his beliefs, and in fact the existence of such people is an endless source of humor and delight to us.

One of the most troubling aspects of the traditional logical conception of folk psychology is that it saddles people with beliefs which they swear they lack. Consider John Perry's famous example of "the messy shopper":[22] A man shopping at a supermarket sees a trail of white powder on the floor. After closer examination of the powder, he concludes that it is sugar and decides that a shopper ahead of him must have a torn sack of sugar, which is leaking, onto the floor. He forms a belief he would express by saying "That man is making a mess." But in fact the sugar is coming from a torn bag in *his* cart, giving rise to following:

(1) John believes that that man is making a mess.

(2) John is that man.

Therefore,

(3) John believes that he is making a mess.

This unacceptable conclusion seems to indicate that folk psychology has an inherent flaw: It disallows a perfectly logical inference. But it is crucial in this debate to separate what we might call the logical conception of folk psychology from folk psychology itself. On the logical conception, the operations on the mental sentences are logical operations. But, the brain seems to act in rather illogical ways in certain circumstances, intimating that it is working according to some other kinds of principles. This invites, then, a view which still holds to the idea of "sentence-sized" units of thought, but posits operations on them different from the typical logical operations, both in the sort of operation which is performed, and in that the computations are probabilistic rather than discrete.

Also, more recent versions of the logical conception are able to assign the correct truth values to the conclusions of such arguments by pointing out that sentences such as (1) and (3) often refer to more than the standard, external referents, such as John, and the mess on the floor.

Eliminativism

Mark Crimmens, for instance, argues that such sentences also make a "tacit reference" to mental representations in the mind of the target person, in this case, John. The conclusion, statement (3), is false because it posits a belief consisting of John's concept of himself and the concept of making a mess, and John in fact has no such belief.[23] He has, rather, a belief consisting of his concept of some other man, and the concept of making a mess. It is important for the proponents of the logical conception to solve this problem in an acceptable way, in order to continue to show that their techniques can treat folk-psychological claims.

An Argument From Confabulation

An argument the Churchlands do not give but might concerns an intriguing neurological phenomenon known as *confabulation*. When certain types of neurological patients are asked questions, they confabulate: Rather than admitting they do not know the answer to the question, they make up a plausible-sounding, but false answer.[24] What is interesting about confabulation is that the patients are not doing this intentionally—they genuinely believe the answers they are giving. Some amnesia patients, for example, when asked what they did yesterday, will describe events which either never happened, or happened long ago. Split-brain patients, whose cerebral hemispheres have been surgically separated in order to prevent the spread of epileptic seizures, will also confabulate in certain experimental settings. For instance, the right hemisphere can be given visual information without the left hemisphere knowing about it. When the right hemisphere responds (by pointing with the left hand), and the patient is asked the reason for that particular response, the *left*, speaking hemisphere will create some plausible but false reason for the response. The falsity of confabulations can be used to cast doubt on the truth of folk psychology—if our reports of our mental states are merely confabulations, this would tend to support the claim that folk psychological self-ascriptions are not correctly describing actual brain events.

We all get a bit confabulatory in certain situations, as Dennett points out:

> There are circumstances in which people are just wrong about what they are doing and how they are doing it. It is not that they lie in the experimental situation but that they confabulate; they fill in gaps, guess, speculate, mistake theorizing for observing. ... They don't have any way of "seeing" (with an

inner eye, presumably) the processes that govern their assertions, but that doesn't stop them from having heartfelt opinions to express.[25]

The existence of confabulation is troubling for the folk-psychological realist, because it presents an image of our unknowingly making up folk-psychological ascriptions. The realist must try to argue that confabulation is the exception rather than the rule, and that correct introspective reports in folk-psychological terms are still possible.

Sentences and Concepts

Folk psychology depicts human thought as an interaction among attitudes such as beliefs and desires, each of which contains about as much information as can be expressed in an average-sized sentence. This explains why folk-psychological verbs so often take a full sentence as their object, as in, "I (see, believe, know, wish, fear) that *we are at war*": Sentences nicely describe thoughts because both sentences and thoughts contain about the same amount of information, structured in the same way. Thus folk psychology makes clear and testable claims about the *size* of the relevant representations involved as the end products of perception, the participants in cognition, the causers of actions, the inhibitors of actions, and so on. The folk-psychological realist argues that the notion that our minds operate with sentence-sized units has tremendous explanatory power. For one thing it explains why the sentence is the standard unit in all of the world's languages. It also explains why there is such a natural breakdown of words in sentences into verb phrases and noun phrases: The typical thought predicates something, some property, action, disposition, etc. (described by a verb phrase) of some object (described by a noun phrase).

This similarity between sentences and thoughts has been pursued to great lengths by some researchers. In the mid-1970s, Jerry Fodor and others hypothesized that there exists something they called the "language of thought."[26] This is a language which all humans *think* in, no matter what external, natural language they speak. The hypothesis of a language of thought contains the idea that thoughts are composed of separate concepts—the rough analog of words in a sentence. My thoughts, for instance, that George W. Bush is the president, and that Bush is from Texas, involve the same concept, of Bush. The claim of a language of thought is friendly to folk psychology since the thoughts it posits are made of concepts, and are sentence-like, just as folk psychology requires.

There are several arguments and sources of evidence for the claim that there is a language of thought which is not the thinker's natural language (such as English):

First, the tip of the tongue phenomenon: We often have the experience of knowing what we want to say, but being unable find the word to express it. This seems to indicate that the thought itself is not represented in a natural language, otherwise to be aware of the thought would entail being aware of its natural language expression. Second, babies and certain higher animals seem to have concepts without possessing a language. The baby in the crib, for instance, has a concept of her mother in that she is able to recognize her at different times. Learning a language presumably involves associating words with concepts one already possesses. Acquisition of language seems to greatly enrich one's set of concepts, of course, but it seems to require the possession of a basic "starter set" set of concepts.

Third, when tested later, we tend to remember only the content or gist of a sentence and not its actual form in natural language. Again, this seems to show that the incoming sentence is 'translated' into the language of thought, and grammatical niceties which do not carry important information are simply dropped. Fourth and last, the relative ease with which natural languages such as English, German, Swahili, or even Chinese can be translated into one another can be partially explained by the language of thought hypothesis: Since the thoughts expressed in these natural languages were all formed in the same language—the language of thought—the translator simply uses the language of thought as an intermediary step in the translation process.

The question of whether there is a language of thought is important for the question of whether folk psychology might be eliminated, because the existence of a language of thought may show that folk psychology sinks deeper into the brain than the thoughts occurring in natural language which we are sometimes aware of. One sort of response the Churchlands might give would be to focus on the "translation" phase, in which beliefs in the language of thought are translated into a natural language. How do we know whether the data structure which is input to the translator is sentence-like? The question of how items in the language of thought relate does not seem to cut either way, since they do participate in certain logical relations, but they also fail to participate in others.

Successor Theories to Folk Psychology

The brain encodes information not in sentences or sentence-like data structures, but in what are called "activation vectors," according to Paul Churchland.[27] The taste of something, for instance, is coded according to how much it activates each of four receptor types on our tongue, the sweet, sour, salty, and bitter receptors. Each taste creates a different activation profile; a sour apple, for instance, would strongly activate the sour receptors while activating the others less so. Such a system is powerful, because it has the capability to represent a huge number of different tastes. Activation vectors are capable of representing more complex things, such as human faces, and ultimately, all sorts of events in the world. They are the real data structures which lie behind our mental lives, not sentence-like structures. Thus, Paul Churchland says,

> You came to this book assuming that the basic units of human cognition are states such as thoughts, beliefs, perceptions, desires, and preferences. ... Human cognition is thus commonsensically portrayed as a dance of sentential or propositional states, with the basic unit of comprehension being the inference from several such states to some further sentential states.... Their universality notwithstanding, these bedrock assumptions are probably mistaken. In humans, and in animals generally, it is now modestly plain that the basic unit of cognition is the *activation vector*.[28]

The brain computes, not by forming inferences from sentence-like structures, but by performing different sorts of operations on these vectors:

> It is now fairly clear that the basic unit of computation is the *vector-to-vector transformation*. And it is now evident that the basic unit of memory is the *synaptic weight configuration*. None of these have anything essential to do with sentences or propositions, or with inferential relations between them. Our traditional language-centered conception of cognition is now confronted with a very different brain-centered conception,

Eliminativism

one that assigns language no fundamental role at all.[29]

But it is not yet clear how different a brain-centered conception would be. Some activation vectors seem close to being concepts, or at least parts of concepts. There is mounting evidence that we recognize objects by gauging their deviation from a prototypical object of that type.[30] For instance, we recognize birds by gauging their nearness to a prototypical bird representation encoded in memory. Perhaps the brain does this by first forming what the Churchlands call a prototype vector.[31] The possibility needs to be kept open, though, that even if something like prototype theory is found to be correct, prototypes might still be comfortably thought of as concepts, in the way that folk psychology currently depicts them. On this view, the visual representation is a significant *part* of my concept of birds. The concept contains other, non-visual parts, including auditory representations of the ways that certain birds sound. Once one has concepts, beliefs, thoughts and other larger representations can be formed, as long as there is some method of connecting the concepts. The folk-psychological realist, then, might argue that concepts are more important to his approach than sentence-like structures, since the latter can be constructed out of concepts.

If concepts are still standing after brain science has matured, this does not automatically vindicate the folk-psychological realist, however. What happens depends on how similar the things that current scientists call "concepts" are to what we originally called "concepts" in our folk-psychological talk. For example, the fact that we still use the word "heat" does not vindicate any folk theories, or early scientific theories, of what its nature is, for instance the theory that the amount of heat a substance has is due to the amount of *caloric* it contains. The surviving notion of concepts would still need to contain many of the features described in Chapter 1, such as the idea that one concept can participate in several beliefs, the idea that the possession of a concept explains how someone is able to identify and re-identify something, and so on.

Interestingly, the Churchlands still see a role for the concept of *representation* in future brain theories. Not all current approaches do: Proponents of dynamic systems theory,[32] for instance, argue that when one actually looks at how neural-net like structures achieve the sorts of computations which allow for real-world behaviors, one does not find clearly demarcated data structures in such systems which can be called representations. Individual activation vectors, however, can still be thought of as representations, on the Churchlands' account.

Conclusion

Folk-psychological realists cannot deny the importance of showing that folk psychology is well connected to brain science in many ways, and will continue to be so for the foreseeable future. This connection would make brain science accessible and useful to ordinary people, because it would be posed in terms they already understand. If folk psychology is going to be eliminated, the realists might claim, there are no clearly visible signs of that happening yet. On the contrary, theorizing in cognitive science makes full use of folk-psychological concepts. Neuroscientists talk about intentions, voluntary behavior, and images as much as they ever did.

One sort of argument sometimes leveled against the Churchlands' vision for what a future replacement would look like is that the particular theories they mention as replacements are new and speculative, and may not be the prevailing theory in ten or twenty years' time.[33] But it is important to keep in mind that what the Churchlands are proposing goes beyond the future success of any particular theories they mention as successors to folk psychology. The same could be said of neuroscientific theories which the Churchlands introduce because of their argued relevance to traditional philosophical problems. More broadly, the Churchlands are showing *what it might look like* to have a scientific theory that is a candidate for succeeding folk psychology, or a scientific theory which sheds light on a classical philosophical problem. They saying, in essence, "*If* this scientific theory is correct, it is a candidate successor theory," or "*If* this theory in neuroscience is true, it has significant implications for philosophy." What makes the mind-body problem, for instance, so difficult is even *imagining* what a fully materialistic theory of the brain might look like. The Churchlands suggest certain theories precisely because they constitute a way to imagine that memory, for instance, or consciousness, or action, might be produced by neurons. These candidate materialist theories of mental phenomena such as consciousness have the huge benefit of being empirically testable; that is their most important feature. Speaking about their neurocomputational theory of consciousness, for instance (see Chapter 4), Paul Churchland says:

It is a real instance of the general kind of unified and systematic reconstruction of the target phenomena that any adequate explanatory reduction must try to achieve. Whether it is true is a secondary question. But it is a candidate for truth, and its acceptance or rejection will depend on how empirical research continues to unfold, not on how things seem to uninformed common sense, nor on ill-founded argument a priori, nor on thinly disguised arguments from ignorance.[34]

If the specific theories they invoke fall by the wayside as science moves on, larger points are still in effect. In this realm at the boundary of neuroscience and philosophy, often the only difference between a theory in neuroscience and a philosophical position is a philosopher bold enough to present the theory as an answer to a philosophical question, that is, as a philosophical theory.

Endnotes

[1] "Replies to Comments" [Symposium on *Neurophilosophy*], *Inquiry* **29** (1987), 247-248.

[2] Personal communication.

[3] Cambridge: Cambridge University Press, 1979.

[4] "Do We Propose to Eliminate Consciousness," in *The Churchlands and Their Critics*, ed. Robert N. McCauley, Oxford: Blackwell Publishers Ltd., 1996, 298-299.

[5] Review of *Scientific Realism and the Plasticity of Mind*, in *The Philosophical Quarterly* **30** (1980), 268-269.

[6] Review of *Scientific Realism and the Plasticity of Mind*, in *Philosophy* **55** (1980), 273-275.

[7] *The Churchlands and Their Critics*, 300.

[8] *Neurophilosophy*, by Patricia Churchland, Cambridge, Mass.: The MIT Press, 1986, 296.

[9] *Ibid.*, 278.

[10] *Ibid.*, 281.

[11] Patricia Churchland, *Neurophilosophy*, 279.

[12] *Ibid.*, 358.

[13] "Folk Psychology," by Paul Churchland. In *On the Contrary: Critical Essays, 1987-1997*, Paul M. Churchland and Patricia S. Churchland, Cambridge, Mass.: The MIT Press, 1998, 7.

[14] *Ibid.*, 7-8.

[15] *Matter and Consciousness*, by Paul Churchland, Cambridge, Mass.: The MIT Press, 1984, 43, italics in the original.

[16] Such realists include John Searle, see *Intentionality*, Cambridge, Cambridge Univ. Press, 1983; Jerry Fodor, see *The Language of Thought*, Cambridge, Mass.: Harvard Univ. Press, 1975; and Terence Horgan and James Woodward, see "Folk Psychology is Here to Stay," *The Philosophical Review*, **94** (1985), 197-220.

[17] These would include Daniel Dennett, see *The Intentional Stance*, Cambridge, Mass.: The MIT Press, 1987.

[18] "Replies to Comments," [Symposium on *Neurophilosophy*] *Inquiry* **29** (1987), 241-272.

[19] *Ibid.*

[20] See Paul Churchland's book, *Matter and Consciousness*, 43.

[21] "Folk Psychology," 8.

[22] John Perry, "The Problem of the Essential Indexical," *Nous* **13** (1979), 3-21.

[23] See *Talk About Beliefs*, by Mark Crimmens, Cambridge, Mass.: The MIT Press, 1992.

[24] See *Brain Fiction: Self-Deception and the Riddle of Confabulation*, by William Hirstein, Cambridge, Mass.: The MIT Press, 2003.

[25] From *Consciousness Explained*, by Daniel Dennett, Boston: Little, Brown, and Company, 1991, 94.

[26] Jerry A. Fodor, *The Language of Thought*, Cambridge, Mass.: Harvard University Press, 1975.

[27] *The Engine of Reason, the Seat of the Soul*, by Paul Churchland, Cambridge, Mass.: The MIT Press, 1996, 21-24.

[28] *Ibid.*, 322-323.

[29] *Ibid.*

[30] See the work of Eleanor Rosch, such as "Principles of Categorization," in *Cognition and Categorization,* eds. E. Rosch, and B. Lloyd, Hillsdale, N.J.: Erlbaum, 1978, 27-48.

[31] *The Engine of Reason, the Seat of the Soul*, 29.

[32] See for example the paper by Timothy van Gelder, "The Dynamical Hypothesis in Cognitive Science," *The Behavioral and Brain Sciences* **21** (1998), 615-665.

[33] See Patricia Kitcher's article, "From Neurophilosophy to Neurocomputation: Searching for the Cognitive Forest," in *The Churchlands and Their Critics,* ed. R. McCauley, Oxford: Basil Blackwell Publishers, 1996.

[34] *The Engine of Reason, the Seat of the Soul*, 223.

3
Neurophilosophy

> *The philosopher is just another theorist, one whose bailiwick often places him or her at the earliest stages of the process by which protoscientific speculation slowly develops into testable empirical theory.*
>
> Paul Churchland, "The Continuity of Philosophy and the Sciences," 1986

Introduction

The central idea behind the neurophilosophy movement created by the Churchlands is that brain science is highly relevant to several classical philosophical issues, such as the mind-body problem. Neurophilosophers all tend to espouse the idea that materialism can develop thorough, powerful, and satisfying theories about the mind by interpreting our knowledge of the brain's biology. As the different sciences of the brain entered a revolutionary era in the late 1970s, the Churchlands and a few other materialist philosophers began poring over the results of the scientists in the hope of finding something of relevance to their ancient puzzles. In the mid-eighties, Paul Churchland reported his findings in *Matter and Consciousness*,[1] a compact, very accessible guide to the current state of the mind-body problem. It included the topics one might see in any philosophical book on the problem: descriptions of the arguments for and against the different competing approaches, such as dualism, materialism, and behaviorism, as well as an examination of folk-psychological attitude reports (see Chapter 1), and of the problems involved in knowing about other peoples' minds. But toward the end of the book was something new, a chapter on neuroscience, complete with several figures of neurons, neural nets, and of the brain. Perhaps more because of its clarity and conciseness than its broaching the topic of the relevance of neuroscience to philosophy, *Matter and Consciousness* was widely adopted as a text. This opening shot was followed two years later in 1986 by the publication of Patricia Churchland's more radical book, *Neurophilosophy*.[2] In different forms, it reinforced several of the themes in Paul Churchland's book, but the forty pages on neuroscience were now expanded to over two-hundred pages on all aspects of current neurobiology in *Neurophilosophy*. *Neurophilosophy* also contained a large section on the philosophy of science, which dealt primarily with the issues involved in reducing talk about the mind to talk about the brain. Together the two books constituted a single, sustained argument to the effect that philosophers needed to attend to what contemporary neuroscientists were discovering.

Outsiders to philosophy may not see why what the Churchlands did was revolutionary, since it seems so natural to study the brain in order to solve the problem of how the mind relates to it. But inside philosophy this move was quite controversial. One might think that in order to understand the mind, materialist philosophers would have long ago dedicated themselves to learning everything they could about the brain. Curiously, this did not happen, although if we look at the recent history of the philosophy of mind, the reasons become clear enough. One reason was a widespread belief among philosophers that someone who counts the findings of scientists as crucial data is no longer acting as a philosopher, but has become a scientist. The Churchlands have challenged this conception of philosophy as far too narrow, invoking philosophy's long history of entanglement with all of the sciences.

Even among philosophers conversant with current brain science, however, there was a widespread tendency to assume that science simply was not ready with the information and theory needed to make a reduction possible. Once the information became available, the assumption was that there would be a smooth reduction of our concept of mind to brain science. These philosophers were allied with the Churchlands in their interest in neuroscience, but the two groups were soon to be at odds on the issue of how exactly the new discoveries relate to folk psychology. Indeed, arguing for the relevance of neuroscience to philosophy would have been much easier to do from the viewpoint of the *realist* about folk psychology. The Churchlands were in the difficult position of arguing that neuroscience is relevant to philosophical problems, just not in the folk-psychological form in which we currently pose them.

Another reason why philosophers resisted learning about the brain was a strange sort of bias against attempting to relate what was going on inside the skull to the external world of behaviors—of talking, of the intricate dance of movements and facial expressions involved in our everyday interactions—known as *behaviorism*. According to the behaviorist, we can come to understand that outer world on its own terms without entering into the world inside the skull, into that odd-looking assemblage of curiously-shaped, dully-colored organs known as the brain, much less worrying about the terminally fuzzy "mind." This idea, that it is a mistake to even try to talk about what we are consciously aware of, was the most powerful idea in psychology and the philosophy of mind in the 20th century, both in terms of what it created and in terms of what it destroyed.

Behaviorism was a long interruption of a movement which sought to bring what is known about the brain into the philosophical realm. Prior to the behaviorist era, thinkers wrote in language which contemporary cognitive scientists would find much more accessible than that of the behaviorists. The great philosopher-psychologist William James, in his book *The Principles of Psychology*,[3] effortlessly moves from philosophical issues about the self, about consciousness, and concepts, to then-current findings in brain science and psychology, as did many other writers of that time. It took a sort of perversity to lead entire disciplines away from such a natural-seeming mix during the several decades in which behaviorism reigned.

The attempt to talk about what goes on in the mind suffers from a deep kind of incoherence, according to the logical behaviorists—the philosophical version of the psychologist's behaviorism. If people are going to describe mental events, their words must *refer* to some definite entity or process in order for the description to be meaningful.[4] There are criteria which must be met, however, before we allow that a person is using a certain phrase to refer to something. For instance, if a two-year old looks at a neighbor's cat and says for the first time, "kitty," we would be tempted to say that when he says "kitty" he is referring to cats. But if he then points at the neighbor, the family dog, and the sprinkler, and says "kitty" each time, we take back what we said. One can only refer to x if one can properly identify x, and distinguish it from not-x, i.e., one must have a concept of x. The problem, then, with conscious experiences is that one has no way to tell whether one is able to correctly re-identify them or not, because there is no check, external or internal. It might seem quite clear to you that the conscious experience you are having now is the same one you had yesterday at this time, but this is not enough, they argued: Seeming is not being.

There is still work to do, primarily in analyzing concepts such as *believe*, *desire*, and *see*, according to the behaviorists. What needed to be done was to uncover the hidden logical structure of the concepts themselves. Much of this seemed to consist of intricately related sets of criteria which phenomena need to satisfy in order to count as a case of believing, thinking, etc. What was uncovered was indeed fascinating, and it did yield many valuable insights into folk psychology, human nature, and human society. But like its cousin in psychology—the behaviorism of John Watson and B.F. Skinner—logical behaviorism excluded other approaches because it was too short-sighted to see that they would pay off a few years hence.

Among mainstream philosophers, there were forays into brain-based materialisms, such as U.T. Place's "Consciousness is a Brain Process" (1956), and J.J.C. Smart's "Sensations and Brain Processes" (1959), but they tended to merely mention the brain without actually bringing facts about its structure and function into their arguments.[5] This was the existing milieu when the Churchlands began their academic careers in the 1970s. In the introduction to *Neurophilosophy*, Patricia Churchland recounts her frustration with the conceptual analyses of the linguistic behaviorists:

> In the mid-seventies, I discovered that my patience with most mainstream philosophy had run out. What had instead begun to seem promising was the new wave in philosophical method, which ceased to pander to "ordinary language" and which began in earnest to reverse the antiscientific bias typical of "linguistic analysis."[6]

When philosophers finally began to move away from behaviorism, however, it was not toward neuroscience, but toward the then-popular artificial intelligence movement. "Even there I had a major misgiving, however," continues Patricia Churchland,

> Because the sciences embraced by the new wave as relevant to understanding the nature of the mind did not include neuroscience. Indeed, the best of what there was had espoused a novel and sophisticated form of dualism....[7]

The main such science was artificial intelligence, which contained a dualism based on the distinction between hardware (analogous to brain) and software (analogous to mind; more on this in the next chapter). Only the software is of philosophical interest here, according to them, since computation theory tells us that programs can run on any sort of hardware at all, including computers made out of sticks and stones. Such theories, she continues,

> dismissed neuroscience as largely irrelevant to theories in psychology and philosophy. Since I was a materialist and hence believed that the mind is the brain, it seemed obvious that a wider understanding of neuroscience could not fail to be useful if I wanted to know how we see, how we think and reason and decide. I therefore decided to find out in detail whether what was already known in neuroscience was of any use in understanding cognitive functions.[8]

One reason for the Churchlands' success in drawing the attention of philosophers to neuroscience is that by including chapters on parallel distributed processing and neurocomputing in *Matter and Consciousness* and *Neurophilosophy* they provided a natural segue from existing work in artificial intelligence. But no doubt another reason behind the success of the Churchlands and the neurophilosophy movement is that they were not the only ones growing impatient with the current state of things in philosophy.

Neurophilosophy reveals that Patricia Churchland has a natural feel for the sciences, and she presents what she learned with great clarity, aided frequently by diagrams, which were then a strange thing to find in a philosophy book. The research and acumen for which details to include and which to leave out in the book's five beginning chapters on neuroscience are impressive. One of the most valuable contributions of the book is the manner in which those first five chapters present knowledge about the brain in a way which is, rather subtly at times, philosophical. The strategy of the early chapters appears to be just to present the information she found relevant to philosophy, and let the reader see the relevance for himself. In the book's introduction, she gives the following list of philosophical questions which brain science might be able to shed light on:

> What sort of business is reduction? What conditions should be satisfied in order that identification of phenomena can be made? How are we to understand in a general way what representation is? How are we to assess the prospects for a unified account of mind-brain function? How might language

relate to the world.[9]

If there were any doubts about Patricia Churchland's expertise in the realm of science, they were answered when *The Computational Brain*[10] appeared in 1992. Written with prominent neuroscientist Terrence Sejnowski, this book was not a mere reporting of findings, but more like the seminal book of the emerging field of neurocomputation. Researchers in this field seek to understand how neurons—the basic cell type found in the brain—can achieve the sorts of computations behind our perceptions and actions. They combine the study of neuroanatomy with the construction of computer simulations of interconnected sets of neurons in order to build their theories.

The Psychology of Philosophers

The neurophilosophy movement was indeed a revolution in philosophy, with all the accompanying hysteria and hard feelings. When they began presenting the view, the Churchlands encountered tremendous resistance from the traditional philosophical community. Without the Churchlands, though, philosophy's inevitable reintroduction to science might have been a lot rougher. Philosophers might have one day just noticed that scientists were working away on *their* problems, without reading their work or citing them at all. The Churchlands, with help from many others, have helped to keep both scientists and philosophers informed of each other's work, and to open up dialogue between the two groups.

One source of suspicion among traditional philosophers toward the Churchlands, one suspects, can be described as follows: Whenever someone investigates a question on which folk wisdom has already weighed in, an intriguing psychological dynamic plays itself out in her mind. There is a standing and powerful motive to find that in fact, things are not as the folk think them to be, but rather quite some other way. Only then does the investigator really have something worthy of people's attention and interest—who cares if she confirms something everyone believed anyway? (This last point is simply a mistake of course, confirmation contains information valuable to a theory, just as disconfirmation does.) As an example of such a disconfirmation, one of the most enduring pieces of information in the mind of anyone who ever took a physics class is the idea that what appear to us to be solid objects in fact consist of a ludicrous amount of empty space. Such exceptions stick in the mind, and some people never tire of recounting them and correcting the uninformed. However, a one-sided diet of too many of these folk-contradictory facts can cause one to become suspicious of scientific theories which are folk-consistent. Worse, such a diet could cause one to come to believe that being folk-contradictory constitutes an argument *for* a theory.

There are philosophers, and even neurophilosophers of whom this accusation is true, but it does not stick well to the Churchlands. One piece of evidence for this is that there are several important folk mental concepts which they still use in their writing and theorizing, because they do not believe they will be, or need to be, eliminated, including *representation, attention* and *visual perception*. There is a selectivity here; they are not urging a simple-minded, wholesale elimination of all mental concepts. One can also see in their work an honest struggle with the question of whether our folk concept of *consciousness* will be eliminated. They discuss its fragmentation, but they also propose a biological theory of consciousness which holds together the most significant features of the folk concept (see Chapter 4).

On the other side among philosophers is a bias toward defending the folk views on an issue, which can range from the simple presumption that the folk view is adequate until proven otherwise, all the way to a pointless clinging to false but familiar ways of thinking. We tend to be this way about our personal belief systems—the mere fact that we hold a belief gives it an initial weight. One reason for this is just that it takes effort and time to revamp one's belief system, and we exercise a natural cautiousness to wait until we are certain such an undertaking it truly justified. This sort of epistemic conservatism may also be at work in the minds of those philosophers wishing to "save" folk psychology.

Another interesting phenomenon which occurs when philosophers become intimately involved in science to the point of actually doing it, is the interplay between the different standards for correctness in science and philosophy. Philosophers in general set this standard at somewhere near mathematical or logical truth. Scientists, on the other hand are more interested in ensuring that their claims are highly *probable*. This probability is typically assessed by statistical techniques, and ranges from a low of 90 to 95% for certain of the social sciences and certain types of experiments, such as those involving very few subjects, up to 99.999% in certain fields, such as physics, or in studies with a large number of subjects. But this probability never reaches the (apparent) 100% certainty available to logical and mathematical inferences.

Many scientists are blessed with a sensitive feel for probability along the entire spectrum, as opposed to the approach of the stereotypical philosopher, which is directed solely at the two ends of the spectrum, 100% and 0% (or 1.0 and 0, in the language of probability theory). Often this type of a philosopher is completely at a loss when probabilities fall inside this range—causing one scientist to joke that, "The only probabilities philosophers know are 1 and 0." This discomfort with science may be one source of resistance among philosophers to the Churchlands' work, since the revolution they are urging would require philosophers to learn about contemporary neuroscience.

This difference in approaches evidences itself strongly when one must determine how damaging an objection is to a theory. In philosophy, a single counterexample to a theory is often enough reason to rework the theory. For instance, if I state that "lying" means, "saying something false," when someone points out that people often say false things by mistake, but are not lying, it is instantly clear that my theory of lying is in need of a major addition. These sorts of cases train philosophers to think that a counterexample to a theory implies that the theory is false, as it stands. When they see clearly how a scientific theory *can* be wrong, and hence cannot attain a mathematical level of certainty, philosophers sometimes devalue the theory by failing to appreciate that it is still superior to its competitors (because it has a higher *probability* of being true). In science, evaluating theories is a complicated and subtle skill. Scientists often must accumulate and carefully weigh different *types* of evidence, for instance, evidence from neuroanatomy about the structure and connectivity of a brain area and evidence from neuropsychology about the behavioral effects of damage to that area.

When they attempt to evaluate scientific theories, philosophers are also prone to confuse amount of detail with the quality of a piece of research, mistakenly assuming that a large amount of detail equals high quality. Again, one needs some sort of broader, more intuitive sense of the significance of the details. Another mistake philosophers make is confusing "big science" with good science. Scientists with large, well-funded projects are able to attract more attention to their results, and able to cloak them in findings based on the latest technologies, the current favorite being a high-resolution brain imaging study. The Churchlands also avoid this criticism. One clear sign of their ability to appreciate small science is their collaboration with the psychologist V.S. Ramachandran.[11] Ramachandran is famous for devising significant experiments using such mundane equipment as a cardboard box or a mirror, relying on creativity rather than expensive machinery.

Two Conceptions of Philosophy

On one conception of philosophy it is impossible for philosophers to have anything to do with scientists, as philosophers. On this conception, philosophy is by definition not science, does not involve itself in empirical experiment or observation, and concerns itself strictly with something called *a priori* knowledge—knowledge not based on experience of the world. Philosophical problems are precisely those problems which can be solved using thought alone. This presumably implies that any problem which is solved by science must not have been a philosophical problem to begin with, otherwise it would have been solved by thought alone long ago. In this section, I will compare this conception of philosophy—which we might call the *armchair conception*—with an alternative I will call the *onion conception*—which is more amenable to the idea that philosophy and science overlap, or are at least continuous with one another.

According to the armchair conception of philosophy, all philosophical problems are solvable from an armchair, using only thought, including conceptual analysis, aided by an occasional "thought experiment." This is because philosophical problems are solvable by attaining *a priori* knowledge, that is, knowledge attainable without experience of the world. This is knowledge attainable *prior* to experience, in contrast with *a posteriori* knowledge, which is knowledge which comes after, or really, from, experience. We do not need experience of the world in order to solve mathematical problems, for instance. You can solve the problem of what 26 plus 19 equals from your armchair, without any help from experience, or from its more regimented version, science. There is also no experience of the world which can refute the claim that the answer is 45.

These definitions of "*a priori*" are either question-begging or unworkable however. Consider the standard definition of "*a priori*": knowledge is *a priori* when it can be attained without experiencing the world. The thought process by which *a priori* knowledge is arrived at always involves observation of a sort, however: One often needs to observe certain properties of one's current thought, for instance, that it is true, or not contradictory. The explicit purpose of a *thought experiment*—a standard philosophical technique—is to envisage a certain state of affairs, then make observations as to the possibility or impossibility of that state of affairs, or its consequences. When we form a conclusion about a thought experiment, we are observing properties of our mental states. To say that this sort of observation is not observation of the world is simply to beg the question against the materialist, because that is precisely what she will say it is. We are discerning physical properties of the brain, on her account. The idea that knowledge which derives from the mind alone is somehow of a different sort depends in this case entirely on dualism about the mind.

Another account of the nature of *a priori* truth is that it is a truth not about our physical world, but about an abstract, non-physical reality, a view known as *platonism*. The sentence "Squares have four 90 degree angles," is true. The sentence is not made true by any squares actually made of matter here on earth, though, since no square on earth has four angles which are exactly 90 degrees. What makes that sentence true, the platonist argues, must be an actual perfect square, perhaps existing in a non-physical (but somehow still spatial!) realm. Patricia Churchland, writing with Rick Grush, objects to platonism on epistemic grounds: "What [is] supposed to be the nature of the interactions between the Platonic realm and the thinker's *brain*?"[12] All other cases of knowledge involve some sort of physical, causal connection between the event known about and the person. The reason why you know that Kennedy was assassinated is that the event itself sent forth causal chains which allowed people to know about it, beginning with the people there with Kennedy, passing from them to others until one of those causal chains reached you. Platonists have never produced a satisfactory account of how we come to know mathematical truths. "Platonism," the Churchlands write, "is surely a kind of convenient myth, rather like the way in which frictionless planes and ideal gases are convenient myths...."[13]

"*A priori*" and "*a posteriori*" might better describe ways of solving problems, than problems, or pieces of knowledge, themselves. Is there such a thing as an *a priori* problem? This may just mean "problem whose most convenient solution technique is *a priori*." After all, one could solve the math problem by venturing out into the world and counting trees. *A priori* and *a posteriori*, on this conception, are two different ways of knowing, not two types of items of knowledge or problem. The difference between the two may be capturable by a future materialism. The primary difference between them is that the senses and cognition are "online" together when knowledge is gained *a posteriori*, whereas the senses are either not functioning in their normal way, or disconnected from cognition when the person is gaining knowledge *a priori*. If human knowledge gaining is a purely physical process, then the account of the gaining of *a priori* knowledge is a scientific problem, just as the account of *a posteriori* knowledge gaining is. The fact that the human brain uses two different processes for grasping problems does not automatically indicate that there really are two types of problem.

Perhaps there is another way to construe the *a priori*/*a posteriori* distinction so as to affirm the armchair conception. Disciplines are identified by whether they gain knowledge *a priori* or *a posteriori* techniques. Mathematics and logic (which is considered by philosophers to be a branch of philosophy) make use of *a priori* techniques. So then, a discipline uses either *a priori* techniques or *a posteriori* techniques, and no mixes of the two are allowed, the upholder of the distinction might argue. But computer science is an exception to this. It has both *a priori* and *a posteriori* components; computer scientists know about software, but they also know about hardware—their primary professional society is called the Association for Computing *Machinery*.

Compare the armchair conception with this alternative.[14] On this competing conception of philosophy, philosophers peel away the unknown layer-by-layer, as one would peel an onion. The word "philosophy" just means, "love of wisdom," and the first philosophers were indeed lovers of any and all wisdom. They studied mathematics, astronomy, engineering, physics, biology, linguistics, meteorology and music. As techniques were developed for solving each type of problem, one-by-one the fields peeled off from philosophy and became separate disciplines. The last discipline to peel away was psychology, which became a distinct field some time around the late 1800s. The picture in general seems to be this: Philosophy was born with man's ability to ask, and his attempts to answer, certain hard questions. At first philosophy contained everything, because every question was a hard question. The discovery of successful techniques makes whole sets of questions answerable, however. The domain of philosophy, then, is the set of significant questions which are currently intractable with the techniques available to us. Philosophers are people who deal with intractable questions which are important to us. This is how the domain of philosophy is to be delineated, not via the *a priori*/*a posteriori* conception, or by an attempt to find a common nature to philosophical problems (other than their intractability and importance) or techniques. On the onion conception, today's philosophical problems have in common only their extreme difficulty. Everything tractable has been handed over to other disciplines, but it was philosophers who made the problems tractable.

According to Paul Churchland, contemporary academic philosophy also misunderstands philosophy's connection to science because of a one-sided diet:

> Philosophy's position relative to the sciences is often obscured by the standard manner in which the history of philosophy is taught. The selected works and passages chosen for the undergraduate student's attention are generally chosen with an eye toward illuminating current philosophical issues. One tends to learn Aristotle's ethics, and his logic, and his theory of perception, for example, in far more detail than his cosmology, or his biology, or his views on space and vacuums, or his theory of motion.... In suppressing or bypassing the clearly proto-scientific elements in Aristotle, we ignore some of philosophy's greatest moments, and we emasculate our own discipline.[15]

Paul Churchland also mentions the physiological writings of Descartes, Berkeley's theory of vision, Kant's work in astronomy, Hume's writings on psychology, and others. Were these scientific endeavors clearly separate from their work in philosophy? In the case of Descartes, to take one example, it is obvious that his scientific speculations about brain anatomy were intimately connected with his thinking about the mind-body problem. One of his reasons for choosing the pineal gland as the crucial place in the brain where mind met body was that it is one of the few organs in the brain which does not come in twos, and Descartes assumed that our conscious mental lives have a unity, not a duality.

This debate, about how close philosophy is to science, and about whether philosophy should define itself by claiming access to something such as *a priori* truth, is at least as old as Aristotle. Guthrie nicely describes Aristotle's scientific approach to philosophy, which was developed partly in response to Plato's positing of perfect Forms, or Ideas—perfect examples of everything found on earth, such as the perfect square mentioned above:

> Philosophy, as it appeared to [Aristotle], was an attempt to explain the natural world, and if it could not do so, or could explain it only by the introduction of a mysterious, transcendental pattern-world, devoid of the characteristic natural property of motion, then it must be considered to have failed.[16]

As Aristotle's case again demonstrates, it is not a coincidence that all these philosophers were also scientists. One suspects that in their minds, classically philosophical ideas were connected via countless lines of thought to classically scientific ideas. No doubt they also could not avoid applying the same ways of thinking and standards to both.

The Churchlands are thus continuing in the more recent tradition of W.V.O. Quine (1908-2000), the logician and influential 20th century American philosopher, who argued that certain branches of philosophy, such as epistemology (the study of knowledge) will become "naturalized," that is, will eventually become scientific rather than philosophical inquiries.[17] "Epistemology, or something like it" said Quine,

> simply falls into place as a chapter of psychology and hence of natural science. It studies a natural phenomenon, viz., a physical human subject.[18]

The onion conception of philosophy is also able to explain why early presocratic philosophers such as Thales, Anaximenes, and Anaximander are regarded as philosophers when they thought entirely about what is today regarded as physics—they were trying to answer the question, What is everything made of? They were philosophers because in their time that question was an intractable question. Philosophers have similarly entered the current debate on how to resolve paradoxes in quantum mechanics[19] simply because the problems are extremely difficult, and no technique has been developed for solving them. To suggest that philosophers have entered that debate only to clear up *a priori* or conceptual difficulties is to limit their vision in a pointless way. It may turn out that the solution to the paradoxes results from the development of a new technology, rather than a mere conceptual breakthrough. Does this mean that those philosophers were somehow deluded as to what they were doing? One might make similar remarks about the mind-body problem. At this point many will agree that it seems quite plausible that a breakthrough in scientific theory might allow for the solution of the problem of consciousness. It is not clear what it would mean to then claim that the problem could have been solved *a priori* without the crucial information gleaned from science.

Philosophers are people who accept problems no one else knows what to do with. They develop ways to solve those problems, sometimes with existing concepts and techniques, and sometimes by inventing new concepts or techniques. Given that the goal is to solve a problem, and not to solve the problem only within the limits of the discipline of philosophy as they are understood, philosophers need to use any information, any concept, any technique they feel might be useful in solving that problem.

The onion metaphor may contain an incorrect assumption, however, since it conveys the impression that the size of that which is unknown is constantly shrinking, which runs contrary our experience in science and philosophy, where each discovery gives rise to a family of its own questions. There nevertheless remains a clear sense in which the philosopher stands at the edge of what is known and attempts to get her mind around a piece of the great unknown. Perhaps another metaphor then: Philosophy is a living scythe, lopping off chunks of the unknown and creating sciences to process them into the known.

The Brain: A Guide for Philosophers

People who like to put together jigsaw puzzles know there is a critical threshold after which the puzzle gets much easier, because the different areas they were working on slowly coalesce into a coherent whole. Something like this is happening today in the cognitive sciences generally, but especially in the neurosciences. Beginning in the 1970s, the neurosciences entered a revolutionary era, which is still gathering momentum. In the same way that smart and pragmatic investors follow basic research in order to discern what sorts of technological applications might be made possible by breakthroughs in the laboratory, smart and pragmatic philosophers should be following brain science, in order to find valuable evidence which bears on philosophical problems. But where to begin learning about the brain, the most complex thing we know of in the universe? One of the most valuable things the Churchlands have done for philosophers wanting to understand the brain is to provide guiding maxims about brain structure and function around which knowledge can accumulate, such as the following:

1. A principle which is a sort of analog in neuroscience to pragmatism in philosophy: "Nervous systems are essentially in the business of motor control."[20] This principle is intended to disabuse those philosophers who might tend to assume that the primary function of the nervous system is cognition. People only think so that they can act more effectively, according to this maxim. The causal chain connecting cognition to motor control can never break, although it can get rather long, especially in the case of us humans. I may see something and not direct any motor activity at that thing for ten years.

In short, the primary function of cognition is to devise problem-solving strategies which can be implemented with the available equipment, i.e., one human body.

2. According to Patricia Churchland, David Hughlings Jackson, the visionary 19th century neurologist

> came to view the brain as an integrated set of systems organized in a hierarchy, with sensorimotor representation featured at every level, but with increasing complexity and sophistication.

The fundamental functional unit of the brain is the perception-action cycle, a continuous chain of processes linking perception, cognition, intention, and action. This is good engineering; it creates a nervous system which is capable of keeping the organism alive despite all types of damage:

> On Jackson's hypothesis, with the destruction of high-level structures the more complicated versions of behavior would also be impaired, but so long as the lower-level structures were intact, simpler "low-level" versions would remain.[21]

The Churchlands hew to this maxim when they describe a simple neurocomputational system, a crab-like entity which can direct its eyes at a target, and use the eyes' positions to direct its hand toward the object.[22] The "crab" has both perception and action, and there is no clear line of demarcation between them (see number 4 below).

3. Processing in the brain is not sequential in the manner imagined by early artificial intelligence theorists and cognitive psychologists.[23] According to this conception, in the case of vision for instance, the brain's processing works only in a "bottom-up" manner, from the detection of edges and contours at the lower levels, leading toward the construction of a three-dimensional visual scene as we are aware of it, as in David Marr's theory, for instance.[24] Contrary to this, what neuroscientists are finding is that processing moves both in a bottom-up and a top-down direction simultaneously. One obvious piece of evidence for this is the way in which our memories of previous interactions with an object affect our current perception of it: An expert car mechanic and a native from the jungles of Borneo do not have the same experience when they look under the hood of a car.

4. There is often no clear distinction between perception and action, contrary to the standard conception. In her 1994 article written

with Terrence Sejnowski and V.S. Ramachandran, "A Critique of Pure Vision,"[25] Patricia Churchland further criticizes the theory of vision generated by the work of Marr. She contrasts Marr's approach, referred to as "pure vision" with an approach she and her co-authors believe is truer to the way the brain accomplishes vision, which they call "interactive vision":

> A pure visionary typically assumes that the connection to the motor system is made only after the scene is fully elaborated. His idea is that the decision centers make a decision about what to do on the basis of the best and most complete representation of the external world. An interactive visionary, by contrast, will suggest that motor assembling begins on the basis of preliminary and minimal analysis. Some motor decisions, such as eye movements, head movements, and keeping the rest of the body motionless, are often made on the basis of minimal analysis precisely in order to achieve an upgraded and more fully elaborated visuomotor representation.[26]

We do not just perceive in order to act. At the same time, we act in order to perceive. It is also wrong to think that action only commences when perception is finished. In most of our waking moments, we are acting and perceiving continuously. But the two basic approaches to vision are not automatically incompatible, it should be noted. There can be a high-level system which trades in highly processed representations, while other, independent systems are at work at lower levels.

5. There is no one single control center in the brain. If there were, one might expect to find it in the frontal lobes, where the highest-level processing takes place. One finds no such place there, however:

> The anatomy of the frontal cortex and other areas beyond the primary sensory areas suggests an information organization more like an Athenian democracy than a Ford assembly line. Hierarchies typically have an apex, and following the analogy, one might expect to find a brain region where all sensory information converges and from which motor commands emerge. It is a striking fact that this is false of the brain. Although there are convergent pathways, the convergence is partial and occurs in many places many times over, and motor control appears to be distributed rather than vested in a

command center....[27]

One problem with this view, however, is that it leaves unexplained the great *unity* in our behavior. We very often do only one thing at a time: When I see a dollar on the ground and reach to pick it up, my attention is focused entirely on the dollar, and huge numbers of skeletal muscles must act in concert in order to achieve this simple act. Perception and motor control work seamlessly together. Is this unity somehow superficial, perhaps imposed upon the brain's output just before it enters the spinal cord? It might be the case that there is no one focal area in the brain where perception changes into action, but this does not imply that there are not large systems, involving many brain areas, which achieve this.

We also present ourselves to others as unified beings. Indeed, this is a requirement for living in a society. One way to see this is to look at cases where the unity breaks down, such as multiple personality disorder, or "alien hand syndrome": This syndrome is typified by an arm engaging in actions outside of the will of the patient, as if it "had a mind of its own."[28] The Churchlands might respond that it is exactly this social pressure to present ourselves as unified that causes an artificial unity to appear in our minds as folk psychology depicts them. There are all manner of different computations going on in our brains at any one time. The fact that folk psychology depicts our mental lives as a unified, serial stream of thoughts merely shows how shallow it is, since we know that all sorts of other things are going on in parallel with what we are aware of.

6. The brain can be studied or thought of at different levels of organization: systems, topographic maps, layers and columns, local networks, neurons.[29] The Churchlands themselves have chosen to enter the debate primarily at the level of systems of neurons. On one hand, this is a natural point of entry into brain science for philosophers, since it emphasizes computation—the sort of thing philosophers understand and are comfortable with. But on the other hand, a more natural way into science from philosophy would begin at the highest level of scientific explanation, i.e., something more like neuropsychology. Neuropsychologists and neurologists write about conditions which are more familiar to us from the point of view of our everyday mental lives. The Churchland's eliminativism may have worked to close off this route to them, however, since sciences at the level of neuropsychology are the sciences still the most riven with folk-psychological terms.

Scientism

Scientism is variously described as the view that science is the most important branch of human inquiry or, in a more extreme version, that science is the only important branch of human inquiry. One never hears the more extreme view any more; it is regarded as abhorrent, because of the assumption that it threatens to reduce the rich variety of techniques used, for instance in the arts, to the stingy but rigorous techniques of the scientist. The Churchlands ascribe to neither of these views, and they make it clear that their goal is simply to bring scientific findings about the brain into certain philosophical debates.

Many of the early cries of "scientism" were directed not at science in general, but at particular conceptions of science popular early in this century, such as positivism and behaviorism. There were indeed quite reasonable objections to those views, based mainly on their narrowness. Certainly no one since the positivists has believed the extreme version of scientism. Positivism, which is the theory that only those claims which have a clearly stated method of verification in terms of simple empirical tests are meaningful, terrorized academia throughout the 1930s. It eventually collapsed onto itself, however, when it was pointed out that the theory itself cannot pass the meaningfulness test, since it is not subject to empirical testing.

It is interesting to note how much of the force behind many cries of "scientism" depends either on outdated worries about behaviorism or positivism, or on an unexamined dualism about the mental. "The scientists are forgetting about human feelings," one often hears. What those currently making this objection have not noticed is that today's materialisms have powerful new hypotheses about the nature of emotions, including their conscious aspects.[30] These theories also contain radical new hypotheses about how vital our emotions are to our higher-level cognition. Their proponents argue that people are less rather than more rational when thought is separated from the emotions. So, if those who cry "scientism" are saying that real and significant phenomena are being left out, their cry ought rather to be "bad science." The whole point of science is to provide satisfying explanations of that which we are interested in, not to ignore them or attempt to explain them away.

One particularly absurd characterization of the issue is that the plan is for scientists to use their current knowledge to pass judgement on ethical issues. This possible problem with science is nothing more than the possible problem with any form of objectivism or absolutism: It can become intolerant. One must keep in mind, however, that objectivisms come in two varieties, narrow-minded and open minded. The principles of good science clearly favor an open-minded approach; those acting intolerantly are not acting as good scientists. In the attempt to demarcate science from non-science, philosophers of science have turned increasingly toward the way scientists themselves act; it may be easier to say what it means to be a scientist than what it means to be a science. A good scientist attends closely to competing approaches, actively tries to disprove his own theories, strives to make his work cohere with well-established findings, does not tend to make *ad hoc* additions to his theory in order to account for apparently disconfirming evidence, and so on.

Another reason behind the charge of scientism among philosophers is a fear that those like the Churchlands are trying to make branches of philosophy into branches of science. One root of this sort of charge is no doubt a belief in the armchair conception of philosophy, accompanied by a failure to understand the sorts of connections between philosophy and science described earlier in this chapter. Philosophers have always been making branches of philosophy into branches of science, on the onion conception.

One current movement which still issues accusations of scientism is postmodernism. The postmodernists often mistakenly believe that critiques of science such as Thomas Kuhn's[31] show that it is not objective, or not capable of getting at the truth. Kuhn argued that science is strongly influenced by social factors, and progresses not so much by the gradual accumulation of knowledge, as by "revolutions" in which new theories win over adherents, often by very unscientific means. The postmodernists' account of what actually happens in science contains a rather obvious reliance on the very view they are criticizing, however. What they typically say is that it is not the true view which wins in disputes between theories, but rather the view with the most power behind it, in the form of more people, or more famous people. But, how exactly do they propose to define "power"? If the idea is that it is the power to affect people's minds only, and hence, in their thinking, not treatable by science, this is again an implicit and undefended dualism. Is not the power in question simply the same power that engineers and scientists talk about when they talk about force? "Political" power ultimately rests on the capability to control and direct force. This means that the postmodernists are assuming the truth of the very view they are questioning, by assuming that power is a real, mind-independent property, exactly as the scientists do.

The Churchlands' faith in science is ultimately nothing more than a faith in the human ability to figure out the world. As we come to understand the world, we change the theories we apply to it. It is not a strange and alien world to us, we already know it because we have been part of it for millennia; materialism points out that we ourselves are a physical part of this physical world. Scientists relentlessly check and test each other's work, urging corrections or sometimes outright rejection of theories found to fail newly devised tests. There is no surer or quicker way to become successful in science than to show that some well-accepted hypothesis or theory is false or at least needs significant correcting. Aside from this built-in check, science employs several other checking procedures to ensure the veracity of results published in the science journals: authors must have met the standards required for an advanced degree, the research itself must be reviewed by experts on that problem, and so on. Thus the enterprise of science builds in a system of checks, which is not perfect but quite powerful at weeding out approaches which are flawed.

Faith in science is not misplaced, because it has made itself into the most trustworthy form of inquiry we have. Wherever they are not checked by facts or other people armed with knowledge, human greed, arrogance, laziness, intolerance, and all the rest will move in slowly and often imperceptibly to make the decisions about which views are more important and should be taught, studied and discussed. The idea of a real external world, substantially independent of our wishes, which contains real facts against which to test our theories, is the best check yet devised against these forces. Those disciplines or research programs which are farthest from this model suffer the greatest from a lack of objectivity and begin to rely instead on fundamentally irrelevant factors, such as the charisma or writing talent of the person proposing the view.

Today's materialism needs to be given the chance to offer its explanations of all manner of phenomena, including art, and human interaction in all spheres. Letting scientists and philosophers think about these tasks task in no way implies that any other approach must be made weaker. The majority of people will be attracted to the view that is most interesting, the view which generates the most significant data and further questions. As science matures, there is the possibility that valuable ways of thinking will be temporarily lost, especially if they seem not to cohere with the current paradigms. But if they are truly valuable, they will return. Scientists are constantly making ethical decisions, as are most of us. The best way to ensure that these decisions are good ones is to inform them by our best conception of the facts, i.e., by science. Now thanks to brain science, we can go even further in ensuring that these decisions are good by coming to understand human decision making processes themselves. Knowing how we *do* think is relevant to knowing how we *should* think.

Endnotes

[1] *Matter and Consciousness*, Cambridge, Mass.: The MIT Press, first published in 1984; revised edition published in 1988.

[2] *Neurophilosophy: Toward a Unified Science of the Mind/Brain*, Cambridge, Mass.: The MIT Press, 1986.

[3] William James, *The Principles of Psychology*, New York: Henry Holt & Co., 1890.

[4] See Ludwig Wittgenstein's *The Blue and Brown Books*, New York, Harper and Row, 1958, and *Philosophical Investigations*, New York: MacMillan Publishing Co. Inc., 1953; and Gilbert Ryle's *The Concept of Mind*, New York: Barnes and Noble, Inc., 1949.

[5] See U.T. Place's article, "Is Consciousness a Brain Process," *The British Journal of Psychology* **47** (1956), 44-50, and J.J.C. Smart's "Sensations and Brain Processes," *The Philosophical Review* **68** (1959), 141-156.

[6] *Neurophilosophy*, ix.

[7] *Ibid.*, ix.

[8] *Ibid.*

[9] *Ibid.*, 4.

[10] Cambridge, Mass.: The MIT Press.

[11] See Patricia Churchland's two articles with V. S. Ramachandran, "Filling In: Why Dennett is Wrong," in *Dennett and His Critics*, ed. B. Dahlbom, Oxford: Blackwell, 1994; and, "A Critique of Pure Vision," also with T. J. Sejnowski, in *Large-scale Neuronal Theories of the Brain,* ed. C. Koch. Cambridge, Mass.: The MIT Press, 1994.

[12] *On the Contrary*, 218.

[13] *Ibid.*, 219.

[14] The onion conception of philosophy was inspired by Bertrand Russell's remarks in *The Problems of Philosophy*, Oxford: Oxford University Press, 1912, 153.

[15] "The Continuity of Philosophy and the Sciences," *Mind and Language* **1** (1986), 5-14.

[16] W.K.C. Guthrie, *The Greek Philosophers*, New York: Harper Torchbooks, 1950, 125.

[17] See Quine's article "Epistemology Naturalized," in *Ontological Relativity and Other Essays*, New York: Columbia Univ. Press, 1969.

[18] *Ibid.*, 82.

[19] See for example Richard Healey's book, *The Philosophy of Quantum Mechanics: An Interactive Interpretation*, Cambridge: Cambridge University Press, 1989.

[20] "Replies to Comments," [Symposium on *Neurophilosophy*] *Inquiry* **29** (1987), 268. See also *Neurophilosophy,* 450-451.

[21] *Neurophilosophy*, 162.

[22] See *Neurophilosophy*, 446-447.

[23] See *The Computational Brain*, by Patricia Churchland and Terrence Sejnowski, Cambridge, Mass.: The MIT Press, 23. See also "A Critique of Pure Vision."

[24] See Marr's book *Vision*, San Francisco: Freeman, Inc., 1982.

[25] In *Large-scale Neuronal Theories of the Brain,* ed. C. Koch. Cambridge, Mass.: The MIT Press, 1994.

[26] "A Critique of Pure Vision," 27.

[27] *The Computational Brain*, 23-24.

[28] See "Two Alien Hand Syndromes," by T.E. Feinberg, R.J. Schindler, N.G. Flanagan, and L.D. Haber, *Neurology* **42** (1992), 19-24.

[29] See *The Computational Brain*, 11.

[30] See for example the work of Antonio Damasio, such as his book, *Descartes' Error*, New York: Grosset/Putnam, 1994; and that of Joseph

LeDoux, such as *The Emotional Brain*, New York: Simon and Schuster, 1996.

[31] See his landmark book, *The Structure of Scientific Revolutions*, Chicago: Univ. of Chicago Press, 1962.

4
Consciousness

> *Explaining the many dimensions of consciousness is a daunting task, to be sure, but it is a scientific task that we can already see how to pursue.*
>
> Paul Churchland, *The Engine of Reason, the Seat of the Soul*, 1996

Introduction

If the hypothesis of materialism is true, some of the brain's many physical states and processes are also *conscious* mental states and processes. But what exactly makes one state a conscious state while another one is not? This raises the related question of how consciousness helps the brain with its task of getting us through the world. In short, what is the function of consciousness? These have proven to be difficult questions for materialists, and this encourages the other side, including dualists. They dwell on those aspects of consciousness which seem most intractable to a materialist approach. How, really, can a physical process contain what we know as awareness?, they ask. Wouldn't this have to be a state which is aware of itself? What could this possibly mean in physical terms?

A much more mild negative conclusion about consciousness could also be defended, a type of eliminative materialism: materialism is still correct, but the concept of consciousness will simply be eliminated. The reason why, on this account, these questions about the exact physical nature and function of consciousness have all been so hard is that they assume a false ontology: some sort of mysterious process which allows for awareness, embodies the contents of awareness, embodies a sense of self, initiates voluntary behaviors, and countless other functions. But alas there really is no such process, because the functions on this list are achieved by many different brain processes. Worse, there is no neat one-to-one mapping from traditional functions to processes. It turns out that our intuitive notion of the different functions of consciousness, obtained partly by introspection and lodged within the paradigm of folk psychology, doesn't match the facts well at all, says the eliminativist.

The question of whether the folk-psychological concept of *consciousness* will be eliminated is apparently one of a few issues on which the Churchlands disagree. In her article, "Consciousness, the Transmutation of a Concept" (1983)[1], Patricia Churchland argues that the concept of consciousness is fragmenting, being disassembled by science into a cluster of inter-related concepts, such as *attention*, *working memory*, and so on. The intuitive sense that events are traceable to a single phenomenon is sometimes mistaken after all, as clearly happened with the folk-psychological concept of *madness*. Paul Churchland, on the other hand, has developed an account of consciousness which keeps together most of its traditional features, while describing them in neurocomputational terms, exactly the way one goes about saving a concept from elimination.

More than any other area, their work on consciousness shows that, while they started as philosophers, the Churchlands have become cognitive scientists, freely bringing theories and findings from several different disciplines into their lines of inquiry. They also pursue the problem of consciousness at several different levels. In the arena of classical philosophy, they have criticized metaphysical arguments about how exactly the mind relates to the brain. In the field of computation, Paul Churchland has proposed a computational theory of consciousness. Finally, they have approached the issue on a neurobiological level, by describing concrete biological theories of consciousness, and by criticizing competing scientific conceptions of consciousness on biological grounds.

The Churchlands are dialectical thinkers; many parts of their larger view come out only in their responses to the other important participants in this debate. They have replied to Daniel Dennett on the issue of whether conscious visual representations are "filled in," and to John Searle on the issue of whether computers can think. They have

Consciousness

also responded to a set of arguments put forward by philosophers who do not believe that consciousness can be captured by the techniques of science: Frank Jackson, Searle again, and Thomas Nagel.

Response to Dennett on Filling In

But how does one study something as subtle yet pervasive as consciousness? One way which cognitive scientists have found fruitful is to study the gaps and edges of consciousness.[2] Or the lack of a gap, where there should be one. Each of your eyes has a blind spot, because there is a place on each retina which has no rods and cones—the optic nerve exits the back of the eyeball there. You can demonstrate the existence of the blind spot to yourself by covering your right eye and focusing your left eye on the star in the figure below:

Figure 3.1: *The left eye's blind spot.* The figure should be about nine inches from your face, but slowly move it nearer or farther until the disk on the left disappears in your blind spot.

One of the amazing things about the blind spot is how *big* it is. You can get a feel for its size by slowly moving the page forward, so that the dot begins to appear on the left side of the blind spot. Then slowly move the page farther away so that the dot again disappears into the blind spot, then reappears on the right side of it. How is it that we are not aware of such a large hole in our visual fields? Two answers have been offered: First, we are not aware of the gap because we are simply not attending to that part of our visual field; second, we are not aware of the gap because the brain's visual processing mechanisms actually "fill it in." These are the respective answers given by Daniel Dennett, and by Patricia Churchland working together with perceptual psychologist V. S. Ramachandran. Dennett (1991) argues that to suggest our visual field is filled in is to be tricked by the *homunculus fallacy*: the idea that vision is like a movie theater in which visual systems present the information coming into the eyes to a little man—a homunculus—watching the incoming visual information (which has been filled in to cover the blind spot) on a movie screen. Based on this movie, the homunculus decides what to do, then activates the body's motor systems. This scenario explains nothing about how we see, however: How does the little man see? Is there a littler man in his head, watching a movie in *there*?

Writing together with V.S. Ramachandran, Patricia Churchland (1992)[3] replies by means of ingeniously devised figures which seem to show the filling in process at work. Close your right eye and focus your left[4] eye on the little square in the figure below, holding the diagram about eight inches from your face. Slowly move the page closer and farther in the eight-inch range until the center of the ring which is on the same level as the square, about two inches to its left, disappears, so that it looks like a solid disk instead of a ring. Since it looks different from all the others, it "pops out" perceptually. But if Dennett is correct, this pop out effect should not happen, since we shouldn't see the ring as a solid dot. On Dennett's view, the ring in the blind spot should not appear to be different from the other rings, because we are ignoring the area where the difference is supposed to be. But it certainly looks different; it looks like a solid white dot.

Figure 3.2: *The pop out effect.*[5] The ring which falls within the blind spot is filled in as a solid disk, and stands out from all the other rings. This demonstrates that filling in is a "positive" phenomenon, and not merely the absence of attention, as Dennett argues.

Ramachandran and Churchland's work has recently been supported by the experiments of neuroscientists Fiorini, *et al.* (1997),[6] who showed that the parts of the visual cortex which topographically correspond to the blind spot do seem to be mimicking the activity of adjoining areas which are mapping genuine information—perhaps part of the neural basis of filling in.[7] The existence of filling in processes does not force the positing of a homunculus watching the visual system's representations, surely, but it does raise the question of why exactly the brain fills in.

Response to Searle on Computers and Consciousness

Can a computer think, or see, or feel pain? Put another way, can we, or should we, apply folk psychology to computers? During the 1970s, researchers in artificial intelligence, working primarily on the East coast at such schools as Yale and MIT, began to claim that their computer programs endowed computers with mental states. At Yale, computer scientist Roger Schank developed a program which could take a short story as input, and then provide answers to questions about the story. Schank then rather boldly claimed that the programmed computer's ability to print out the answers shows that it *understands* the story.

This movement in artificial intelligence had a parallel movement in philosophy, known as Turing machine functionalism.[8] Coupled with the new and powerful theory of functionalism, the claims of computers having mental states were much more than just loose talk on the part of some AI researchers. They were part of a large new paradigm for understanding the mind: the computer metaphor. On the West coast, however, philosophers such as John Searle and Hubert Dreyfus[9] brought out arguments against the idea that computers can think or understand. In 1980, Searle published an argument against that claim which came to be known as the Chinese room argument.[10]

If we suppose that Schank's programmed computer is able to answer any question put to it, the problem for Searle was that of somehow getting inside the computer to show that, in spite of its correct behavior, it lacks true understanding. It is an important fact about computers and computer programs that virtually any physical computing machine can run (or *instantiate*) any computer program. According to the artificial intelligence theorists and the functionalists, what is important in producing mentality is contained solely in the program. The particular physical realization of the program is unimportant—a claim I will refer to as *realization independence*. Just about any physical object can be used as a computer, including collections of beer cans, water pipes, or the silicon-based computers we prefer today. Also, however, a human being can be a computer, and it was this possibility which gave Searle what he wanted: In order to know for certain whether the computer is actually understanding, *we can be the computer.*

Searle envisaged a scenario in which he is in a room with a large computer program written to allow whatever follows it to understand Chinese. Outside the room expert speakers of Chinese write questions, in Chinese characters, on slips of paper and insert them through a slot in the door. Searle takes the questions and writes out an answer by following his program, which has sentences in it such as: "If the first character is 乞 and the second character is 乏 then write ڡ," and so on. Outside the room the experts agree that whatever is inside the room understands Chinese, based on the fact that the answers are uniformly grammatical, meaningful, correct, and appropriate. It seems quite clear, however, that Searle understands no Chinese; He still has no idea what any of the characters mean. It seems equally clear that a standard computer in the same situation is doing what Searle is doing, simply matching character forms and spitting out whatever is contained in its program's "write" statements.

One line of response the Churchlands give points to the extreme lengths of time it would actually take a person to follow such a program.[11] Perhaps, in spite of the claim of realization independence, the speed with which computers follow programs *is* relevant to the question of whether a certain programmed computer has mental states. Sometimes the speed at which a machine operates is the crucial element in allowing it to perform a given function. Flapping your wings slowly doesn't produce flying, but flapping them really fast can do the trick. This reply deviates from the classical, more abstract approach to AI though, in which the programs are vital, while the particular speed at which they run is a peripheral issue. Perhaps the best response to the speed reply is simply to put the burden on the Churchlands by asking them to explain why exactly speed matters here. Speed doesn't seem to affect whether a computer is *adding*, for instance. We just allow that some computers add much faster than others.

There is a surprising amount of agreement between the Churchlands and Searle when it comes to saying what it is the computer scientists are doing wrong. They agree in rejecting the assumption of realization independence:

> We, and Searle . . . agree that it is also very important *how* the input-output function is achieved; it is important that the right sorts of things be going on *inside* the artificial machine.[12]

Despite early optimism, the classical approach to artificial intelligence has not been able to produce the sorts of programs their authors so hoped for. For instance, there is as yet no satisfactory program for translating one language into another. The computations involved in getting a robot to navigate around a room using cameras also proved to be far more complex than was first imagined. "The emerging consensus on these failures," say the Churchlands,

> is that the functional architecture of classical [symbol manipulating] machines is simply the wrong architecture for the very demanding jobs required.[13]

The Churchlands note that there are some clear signs that the brain is computing in a very different way from classical computers.

Matching the broad size of the human visual input channel, for instance, strained the computers:

> Realistic results required longer and longer periods of computer time, periods far in excess of what a real visual system requires. This relative slowness of the simulations over the real thing was darkly curious; signal propagation in a computer is roughly a million times faster than in the brain, and the clock frequency of a computer's central processor is greater than any frequency found in the brain by a similarly dramatic margin. And yet, on realistic problems, the tortoise easily outran the hare.[14]

This sort of reply might equally be taken to be a criticism of the willingness of the founders of computer science to let just about anything count as a computer—realization independence. Certainly just about anything can be *used* a computer, but only certain things are *useful* as computers. Searle and the Churchlands agree that in these issues, it is vital not to gloss over the physical architecture of the machine.

In addition to their criticisms of Searle's Chinese room argument, the Churchlands have criticized his views on the nature (i.e., the ontology) of mental states. There are at first some apparent differences between Searle and the Churchlands which dissolve upon a closer reading of Searle, so that, as with the Chinese room, the two sides are not as far apart as might appear. Paul Churchland says that Searle argues that "mental states and activities are not themselves *physical* states of the brain."[15] But Searle is clear that he does regard conscious states as physical. He says, "consciousness is a ... physical property of the brain."[16] Paul Churchland also asserts that according to Searle, "one cannot be wrong about the nature of the contents of one's own mind." According to Churchland, this view "has by now been so thoroughly discredited that it is plain curious to find a philosopher of Searle's prominence still clinging to it." To see that this doctrine is false, he says,

> Consider one's desires, fears, and jealousies. We are not only unreliable in appreciating some of our own desires, fears, and jealousies, we are famously unreliable about them. Clearly then, we are not infallible in our judgements about all mental states.[17]

But Searle also rejects the thesis of incorrigibility, and gives a very similar example:

> If you think about it for a moment, the claim of incorrigibility seems obviously false. Consider Sally [who was earlier wondering how much she loved Jimmy] and Jimmy. Sally might later come to realize that she was simply mistaken when she thought she was in love with Jimmy; that the feeling was incorrectly ascribed; it was in fact only a form of infatuation. And someone who knew her well might know from the beginning that she was mistaken.[18]

The real differences between Searle and the Churchlands lie elsewhere. They clearly differ on the topic of how reliable introspection (or what Searle calls "the first person point of view") is. Searle's most important arguments rely on introspection, while the Churchlands have little trust in it, especially when it occurs in the context of folk psychology. Their disagreement about the import of the Chinese room scenario comes down to this. Searle is arguing that he knows from his own case that he is not understanding, whereas the Churchlands deny that this evidence is important, but argue that classical artificial intelligence is flawed for other reasons.

One suspects the main source of the disagreement between Searle and the Churchlands has to do with Searle's belief that, where conscious states are concerned, to be is to be perceived. According to the normal way of thinking of perception, the objects we see have their own existence, which is completely independent from us or our acts of perception. But theories of introspection which model it on perception are mistaken, according to Searle:

> Where conscious subjectivity is concerned, there is no distinction between the observer and the thing observed, between the perception and the object perceived. The model of vision works on the presupposition that there is a distinction between the thing seen and the seeing of it. But for "introspection" there is simply no way to make this separation. Any introspection I have of my own conscious state is itself that conscious state.[19]

Conscious states are the only physical states of which Berkeley's dictum, "to be is to be perceived" is true, on Searle's account. Any other option would require a distinction between the conscious state and our introspection of it, and "we cannot make this distinction for conscious states."[20] This leads Searle to create a special ontological category for conscious states. What he calls "ontologically subjective" properties of the brain are capable of containing their own awareness, on his conception, and in this respect they are quite different from the other physical properties. The Churchlands, perhaps justifiably, cannot fathom the particular way in which the epistemology and the ontology of conscious mental states are supposed to be tangled together.[21]

Indeed, many thinkers are stymied by what they perceive as states which are simple, in the sense of not being analyzable into parts, yet contain awareness of themselves. More normal cases of awareness involve two components, a being who is aware, and an object or event which she is aware of. We can consider the object separately from our awareness of it, that is, we can separate the metaphysical nature of that object from our particular form of epistemic contact with it. Not so with conscious states according to Searle, they are unique, metaphysical/epistemic simples. But the thought of a single, simple event or state which contains its own awareness produces a mental cramp. We are by definition not allowed to analyze this any further, so we must stop here and proclaim that such events simply exist, and that we have to add them to our ontology—our theory of what kinds of things exist—as Searle does.

In their article, "Recent Work on Consciousness: Philosophical, Theoretical, and Empirical"(1997)[22], the Churchlands criticize a view they describe as positing qualia which are

> (i) metaphysically simple and (ii) exclusively subjective, whereas any physical reconstruction of them would have to be (i) based on causal/relational structures and (ii) entirely objective.[23]

The Churchlands' response is to point out both that introspection is highly fallible and highly incomplete, so the admitted fact that our qualia present themselves to us as simples ultimately carries little weight:

> We must concede, I think, that the quale of a pain, or of the sensation of red, or of the taste of butter, certainly *seems* to be simple and without hidden structure. ... But we are here in danger of being seduced by that favorite of freshman logic classes: an Argument from Ignorance. That we are *unaware* of any hidden structure in the qualia of our sensations, that we *do not know* how our conscious awareness manages to discriminate among different sensations, these admitted facts about our own *lack* of knowledge do not entail that such qualia

must therefore be free of underlying structure, nor that our first-person recognition of such qualia does not depend on some mechanism keyed to the relational features of that underlying structure.[24]

The antireductionists will no doubt reply that any physical properties posited to be part of this underlying structure are merely *correlates* of conscious experience, and in no way capture the conscious events themselves. The Churchlands' last word on the matter involves an appeal to one of their bedrock assumptions, the idea that questions such as these are now also empirical questions:

> "Whether qualia have [simplicity] is a matter for ongoing research to discover, one way or the other, not a matter on which partisan enthusiasts can pronounce from the armchair.[25]

One suspects, however, that the mind-body problem is insoluble if it is posed in terms of such simples. Their theorists seem to recognize this; their typical approach is to argue that we are forced to assume the existence of such simples because of the apparent fact that science can never know my conscious states in the immediate way in which I know them. Just as the question of what the nature of heat is cannot be answered if the answer must make the assumption that heat is a fluid, the problem of the nature of mental states is insoluble, if you assume or employ these metaphysical/epistemic simples. Here is a closer analogy: The problem in early chemistry of how atoms of different types either bond or not is insoluble if you assume that atoms are metaphysical simples. Once you allow that atoms have parts, protons, neutrons, and electrons, you have a framework in which to pose explanations, and countless new roads of inquiry and experiment open up. This sort of consideration might lead one to go back and again explore the possibility of dividing up the existence of conscious states from our knowledge of them.[26]

Response to Jackson on Qualia

The Churchlands have entered another fray surrounding attempts to show that either dualism or materialism is the correct metaphysical theory of the mind. On the side of the dualists, Frank Jackson (1986)[27] has offered what has come to be known as the *knowledge argument* against the exhaustiveness of physical theory. He imagines the following near-future scenario: Mary is a brilliant neurophysiologist who knows about all of the physical facts involved in human color perception, including everything about the brain states and processes that take place in a normal human perceiver when she sees something red. The unusual aspect of the story is that Mary herself has never seen any colors: Her world has been limited to black and white—everything she has ever seen has either been through a black-and-white video monitor or on a white page printed in black ink, and so on. (One must also assume that she has not seen her skin or cut herself, that her clothes as well as the walls of her living space are white, gray, or black, etc.) Finally Mary is taken out of her achromatic prison and allowed to see the multihued world for herself. Jackson's point is that Mary learns of a new fact when she sees red, a fact she did not know even though she was aware of every physical fact involved in such events. Hence knowing all the facts available to physical theory is not knowing all the facts, and it follows that physical theory is not a theory of everything.

Jackson's argument can be depicted as follows:

(1) Mary knows about all of the physical facts of vision.

(2) Mary does not know everything about vision.

Therefore:

(3) There are more facts involved in vision than the physical facts.[28]

Paul Churchland argues in response that Mary does not learn a new fact, but rather learns a new way of representing an existing fact. In actually seeing green grass and red roses she is able to add to her epistemic repertoire a new way of representing the same thing she already understood, i.e., color experience. We often represent facts in two different ways, for instance, a film of the Hindenburg disaster and a written description of the same event. Mary still knows everything there is to know about vision—she knows about all the facts—so this again implies that the second premise is false. Mary just does not represent all the facts in all ways there are to represent them, and there is no reason to think she needs to.

It is not clear that the first premise should be accepted, however. Facts themselves are concrete parts of the physical world. Representations must be physical things on the materialist view, since everything that exists is a physical thing. And when a representation in the brain successfully represents an object in the world, a larger fact comes into existence, that x represents y. So learning about a new way of representing something must be learning about a new fact; it is learning about a new class of properties which normally represent other properties. But aren't the facts involving these things facts about human vision? They are not merely *a* way one can represent something, but *the* way that the human visual system represents something. If so, this implies that the *first* premise of the argument is false—since Mary did not know about a fact which is highly relevant to vision.

Response to Nagel on Introspection

In *Neurophilosophy*, Patricia Churchland examines a set of arguments she "extracted" from Thomas Nagel's influential paper "What is it Like to Be a Bat?,"[29] which also appear to support dualism, including the following:

(1) My mental states are introspectively known by me as states of my conscious self.

(2) My brain states are not introspectively known by me as states of my conscious self.

Therefore (by Leibniz' Law)[30]

(3) My mental states are not identical with my brain states.

The basic template of this argument is:

(1) a is F.

(2) b is not F.

Therefore:

(3) a is not identical with b.

The problem with this argument is not with its form, but rather that the second premise simply begs the question at issue—the Churchlands will deny that premise. When one is introspecting, one *is* learning about brain states, even though it does not seem that way. As Patricia Churchland says, "identities may obtain even when we have not discovered that they do."[31] Philosophy has its set of favorite examples of these cases. The ancient Babylonians called the brightest heavenly body in the morning sky "Hesperus," and the brightest heavenly body in the evening sky "Phosphorus," not knowing that in both cases they were looking at the same thing, the planet Venus.

The Churchlands make important additional criticisms of two similar arguments which employ the notion of *qualia*. Qualia are the properties of mental states which we are (or can be) consciously aware of, for instance, when you imagine a blue square, you are aware of two properties, or qualia: blueness and squareness. Dualists argue that qualia are not physical properties, whereas materialists either argue that qualia are a type of physical property, or that qualia, if they are by definition non-physical, do not exist. One class of argument devised by the dualists points out the (apparently) different ways we can gain epistemic access to qualia and to brain states:

(A)

(1) The qualia of my sensations are knowable to me by introspection.

(2) The properties of my brain states are not knowable to me by introspection.

Therefore:

(3) The qualia of my sensations are not equal to the properties of my brain states.

The next argument is a mirror-image version, posed in terms of the "external senses," such as vision.

(B)

(1) The properties of my brain states are knowable by the various external senses.

(2) The qualia of my sensations are *not* knowable by the various external senses.

Therefore:

(3) The qualia of my sensations are not equal to the properties of my brain states.

The Churchlands will again disagree with the second premises of these arguments, but Patricia Churchland claims that they have an additional flaw. Arguments (A) and (B) commit *the intentional fallacy* according to her: they treat intentional, mind-dependent properties as if they were genuine properties of the objects:

These arguments fail because being-recognized-as-a-something or being-believed-to-be-a-something is not a genuine feature of the object itself, but rather is a feature of the object *as apprehended under some description or other* or *as thought about in some manner*. Having a certain mass is a property of the object, but being-thought-by-Smith-to-have-a-certain-mass is not a genuine property of the object. Such queer properties are sometimes called "intentional properties" to reflect their thought-mediated dependency. Notice that in (B) the property is being-knowable-by-the-various-external-senses, and in (A) the property is being-known-by-me-by-introspection. Both are sterling examples of thought-dependent properties.[32]

Thoughts are more properties of the thinker, than of the object of thought. But if the problem is that it is not clear whether the properties involved really are properties of those objects, perhaps the argument can be recast so that it is not in terms of properties. Instead, we can talk about categories of things—such as the category of qualia and the category of physical brain properties, such as the charge, chemical composition, mass, etc. of neurons. We can describe these categories without making any presuppositions about their relations, for instance, it is still completely open that the category of qualia may be a subset of the category of physical brain properties, as on a materialist account. There is similarly a category of facts which we can learn about by way of introspection. We can also posit a category of facts which can be known about with the external senses, again, leaving it open that this category might include all facts.

(A)

(1) All [qualia] are [knowable by introspection].

(2) No [physical brain properties] are [knowable by introspection].

Therefore,

(3) No [qualia] are [physical brain properties].

(B)

(1) All [physical brain properties] are [knowable by the external senses].

2) No [qualia] are [knowable by the external senses].

Therefore,

(3) No [physical brain properties] are [qualia].

The focus is still on the second premises. They contain what we might call an objective/subjective ambiguity: From my subjective point of view, introspection seems not to reveal physical properties, and it seems that my qualia are forever locked inside me, not accessible to any outsider, especially not via external senses such as vision. To put it another way, when I introspect, I do not experience my qualia *as* brain states. And when I observe your brain from the outside, e.g., via fMRI, I do not experience your brain states *as* qualia. This means, among other things, that I can observe your qualia by observing your brain (objective), but I cannot apprehend them in the particular way that you can (subjective). The Churchlands are arguing that the second premises are false objectively, but they accept the idea that they are true, taken subjectively.

Both materialists and dualists can agree that brain states have two types of properties, mental properties and physical properties. The (property) dualist argues that these two property types belong to two irreducibly different property classes, the mental and the physical. The materialist argues that both types of properties are types of physical properties. Both sides can agree that, to each class of properties, there seems to correspond a way of knowing: Mental properties correspond to introspection, while physical properties correspond to the external senses. The Churchlands seem to accept this way of dividing things. Paul Churchland says that one has "proprietary" ways of knowing about one's own conscious states:

> No matter how much a scientist might know about the current state of your bladder, down to the last stretched cell and cramped muscle fiber, he will not know it in the way that you know it.

The existence of these two, separate ways of knowing does not imply that either way of knowing involves non-physical properties, this is still a materialism:

> Does the correctness of each of these statements mean that the bodily phenomena involved are somehow beyond the explanatory reach of physical science? Clearly not. These phenomena are paradigmatically physical. But it does mean

something. It means that each person has a self-connected *way of knowing* about his own current physical condition....[33]

But again, Paul Churchland agrees that there is a barrier between these two ways of knowing, speaking here about Nagel's bat:

> The intrinsic character of those sensory states will indeed be discriminated and represented by the bat, using its autoconnected pathways, in highly specific ways. And our collective scientific enterprise will not detect or represent them in those highly specific and proprietary ways, although it will indeed both detect them (with microelectrodes) and represent them (in the language of science).[34]

The somatosensory pathways are autoconnected—they always connect us to ourselves, whereas the visual pathways are heteroconnected, they connect us to a wide variety of objects that we see. Paul Churchland is clear that the autoconnected and the heteroconnected ways of knowing have "as the objects of knowledge, exactly the same robustly physical things and circumstances."[35] But do they detect the same *properties* of those things? The answer seems to be no, that the scientist observing my brain from the outside cannot actually sense the redness I am currently imagining.

But if the two ways of knowing have the same objects, this implies that the knowledge events involved share an object, presumably in such a way that a clear line can be drawn between the object and the rest of the knowledge event. This seems to open up the interesting possibility of "crossing the connections."[36] I might be able to know about what your body feels like by hooking up our nervous systems. This implies that the scientist in the above example *will* be able to know about the way your bladder feels to you. Couldn't we simply set up a "shunt" so that the nerves connecting bladder and brain in person A are connected instead to the brain of person B? Thus, we can explore the idea that science need not rely only on the external senses.

Someone might respond that B is not really gaining access to the conscious experience of discomfort which A is feeling. As the example of phantom limbs shows—almost everyone who has a body part amputated experiences a vivid (and sometimes quite lasting) sensation that the limb is still there[37]—the conscious experience of one's body is in the brain, not actually in the body part. Can a case be set up where one person experiences exactly what another is experiencing, given this? There seems to be a problem: The only thing which made the shunt example plausible at all is that there were two things, brain and bladder. Now, the problem is that if there are not *two* things, there are not two things to separate. Even if there are two things to separate, the conscious state still seems to be in either A or B, so one of the two will not be experiencing the correct conscious state, which means that B is not experiencing the conscious state of A. If there were some way to produce a single conscious state spanning both A and B, this might provide a plausible case in which B knows about A's conscious experience in the same way that A knows about it.

It is exactly here where we are halted if we hold a view of qualia as simples, as we saw earlier that Searle does, for instance. Since there is nothing to divide in the case of a simple, any particular quale must exist only in a particular person's mind. But in any conscious state which is realized in the brain there must be some process which allows for the entirety of the conscious state to exist at the same time. Conscious mental states are complexes of many different types of qualia from many different brain areas. There needs to be some physical process which synchronizes the activity of these different states and allows them to function as a single conscious state. Later in the chapter, we will explore one theory of *binding*, a theory about how the brain achieves the blending of many different brain states into a single, unified conscious state. But if binding does happen, if spatially separate brain areas can be bound together and become part of a single conscious state, why can't brain areas in two different people's brains be bound, to allow them both to be aware of at least some of the same qualia? Then one person *could* use introspection to know about another person's qualia.

But if I can use introspection to know about your qualia, does this mean that introspection is not really an "internal sense"? This forces us to make interesting distinctions and clarifications about exactly which way the internal/external distinction is being applied here. We might say that an internal sense is *normally* autoconnected, while the external senses are *normally* heteroconnected. But just as we can make our vision autoconnected by looking at ourselves in a mirror, we can make our introspection heteroconnected, by being aware of the qualia of others. But even if I can experience your qualia via introspection, this would not be a case of me gaining access to your autoconnected perspective via my heteroconnected ways of knowing, and this perhaps was what Paul Churchland was claiming is not possible in the quotations above. For instance, I would not be learning about the way your pain feels by looking at it. Rather, we are making use of my autoconnected pathways. Perhaps even this apparent barrier can be crossed, however.

Introspection normally involves autoconnected pathways; it normally yields knowledge about oneself. But it is interesting that the equipment used by the visual imagination appears to include equipment also employed by vision. One early indication of this came out when psychologists showed that people will mistake a faint image projected onto a wall for their own mental image.[38] Now we can see via different brain imaging techniques that when people are given problems which require mental imagery to solve, visual areas are active. When I imagine myself looking out over the Pacific Ocean, then, I am using certain of the retinotopic maps also used by normal visual perception. This suggests a way in which another person might be able to know about my qualia using her external senses. Suppose we project the contents of my retinotopic maps onto a screen for all to see. This may involve quite a few technical problems—we will need to figure out how to combine the information from different maps into a single image (a problem the brain solves by binding them); and we will need to determine an algorithm for translating activation in certain maps into colors on the screen. But since imagination is vision-like, exactly what someone is imagining may be knowable via the external sense of vision.

Response to the 'Quantum Consciousness' Theories

After a long period in which only the brave opposed behaviorism and wrote about consciousness, lately it seems everyone is writing a book about his or her solution to the problem of consciousness, i.e., the mind-body problem. Certain physicists have postulated that consciousness exists at a much lower level than has been thought, far below the level of neurobiology, at the level of quantum mechanical phenomena.[39] In general, these approaches have not won many converts, although they have attracted some public attention. Patricia Churchland has criticized them, as well as other contemporary theories of consciousness which ignore neurobiology; their theorists suffer from what she calls "brainshyness."[40]

The persistence of the quantum consciousness theorists does force an interesting question, the question of what *level* the phenomenon of consciousness exists at. Or level*s*—getting a useful and satisfying understanding of something typically involves grasping it at more than one level. Autism, for instance, can be seen even at this early point to involve phenomena at the genetic, neurochemical, neurobiological, neuropsychological, psychological, and philosophical levels.

Neurobiology itself contains several different levels of analysis (see Chapter 3). Science typically favors the level at which a phenomenon is most easily understood and manipulated. Cancer, for example, is most frequently understood at the cellular level, even though it includes phenomena at many other levels. To view these as functional levels is to sanction questions about which level a given function emerges at. And this again forces us to ask difficult questions about what exactly the function of consciousness is.

Patricia Churchland is suspicious of the physicists' lack of interest in the biology of the brain. One must admit that it is rather convenient for the physicists who began looking for consciousness to find it right at home, within physics. They did not have to go through a long apprenticeship in the neurosciences, as the Churchlands did. Similarly, cognitive psychologists find their answer within cognitive psychology, computer scientists find their answer within computer science, and so on. Patricia Churchland sees in the quantum consciousness theories a tacit fear of the idea that something as mundane as the biological properties of neurons can explain something as amazing as consciousness and the sense of self, and a resulting tendency to seek refuge in what is just a very fancy dualism:

> Quantum physics, on the other hand, seems more resonant with these residual dualist hankerings, perhaps by holding out the possibility that scientific realism and objectivity melt away in that domain, or the even thoughts and feelings are, in the end, the fundamental properties of the universe....[41]

We relieve ourselves of the burden of explaining consciousness by making it a basic, unexplained property of the universe, present in all matter, an ancient view known as *panpsychism*. The biological approach stands in clear contrast to this. According to it, consciousness is a high-level, biological property of very complicated nervous systems, and is no more likely to be found in a rock than digestion or photosynthesis.

The theories of the physicists are difficult, although this may be what attracts some people to their approach. One reason for the success of the quantum mechanical approach in attracting attention might be the assumption that the solution to a problem as difficult as the mind-body problem must involve a lot of very difficult theories and steps of reasoning. But, given that the most obvious candidate level for a theory of consciousness is biology, we need some reason to direct our attention toward physics, some sort of interesting preliminary result.

Patricia Churchland says,

> The details of the Penrose-Hameroff theory are highly technical, drawing on mathematics, physics, biochemistry and neuroscience. Before investing time in mastering the details, most people want a measure of the theory's "figures of merit," as an engineer might put it. Specifically, is there any hard evidence in support of the theory, is the theory testable, and if true, would the theory give a clear and cogent explanation of what it is supposed to explain?[42]

Outsiders who want the attention of mainstream scientists must do something to grab it. There are a number of ways they can do this: They can engage them in debate at e.g., conferences, they can submit papers to science journals, where they will be carefully read and refereed. But the best way to get the attention of scientists is to use your theory to generate a prediction that no existing theory would make, then show that prediction to be correct.

In an article written with her former student, Rick Grush, Patricia Churchland issues further challenges to the quantum mechanical approach.[43] Many of the challenges focus on a failure of the physicists to explain how the quantum mechanical phenomena they describe can amplify their energy in order to produce effects at higher levels (see the section on reduction in Chapter 2):

> Even if the interesting quantum events did occur in a single tubule, to play a role in consciousness the effect must be transmitted from one tubule to its microtubule neighbor within the cell.... The next-stage-up problem has the same form: to play a role in consciousness the effect must be transmitted from one *neuron* to other neurons.[44]

The situation is as if someone claimed that cars move due to the strong magnetic forces in the aluminum atoms making up the engine block. Certainly the strong forces present in those atoms contain a great deal of energy, enough to move a car. What is missing, however, is an account of how that energy is controlled, how it is amplified and channeled into the work of moving the car. Similarly, if one is arguing that certain physical states can be taken as information which is involved in some computation, one needs to show how the system involved manages those states, i.e., takes certain measures to preserve them, has them interact in certain ways with other physical states, connects them in certain ways to perception and action, and so on. At the biological level, the large topographic maps in the cortex are far better candidates for being among the brain's primary representations used for computation. Their basic connections to perception and action are well understood at this point; there are several well developed theories about how different maps, e.g., sensory and motor somatotopic maps, interact during the execution of "simple" actions such as reaching for a cup.

Prototype of a Neurobiological Theory of Consciousness

There is general agreement among materialists that the process of consciousness, wherever it is in the brain, must involve the cortex, the large gray, wrinkled outer covering of the brain. One of the main reasons for this has been the discovery in the cortex of numerous map-like data structures, including *somatotopic* maps: maps of the body; *retinotopic* maps: maps of the retina, *tonotopic* maps: maps of the sounds detected by the cochlea. The obvious hypothesis here is that conscious states say, involving the body, involve activity in somatotopic maps. One of the great obstacles to this approach, however, is that there are many such maps, and conscious experience presents a single, unified experience, not a disjointed set of representations. In vision, for instance, one retinotopic map represents the colors present in the visual field, while other maps represent the shapes of objects. Some process in the brain is responsible for binding these different representations into one conscious state. The task of discovering this process and explaining how it works has become known as the *binding problem*.

One way that different brain areas might be bound is by participating in a common causal process. One sort of common process binds different cortical areas by sending a synchronizing electrical pulse through them. Neurophysiologist Rodolfo Llinas argues that a part of the thalamus (a set of large nuclei underneath the cortex) known as the intralaminar nuclei regulates such oscillations which unify different parts of the cortex.[45] As Paul Churchland describes it, Llinas and his colleagues found

> small but steady oscillations in the level of neural activity in any area of the cortex, an oscillation of about 40 cycles per second. Llinas found these gentle oscillations at the same frequency in every area of the cortex. Moreover, the oscillations in distinct areas all stood in a constant phase relation to each other: they were all tapping time, as it were, to

a common orchestral conductor. This phase-locked activity indicates that in some way they must all be parts of a common causal system.[46]

Paul Churchland offers a theory which is consistent with and augments Llinas' approach, a theory of what is happening inside the parts of the cortex unified by the oscillations. The different levels of the cortex may be achieving computations and consciousness by acting as a recurrent neural net.

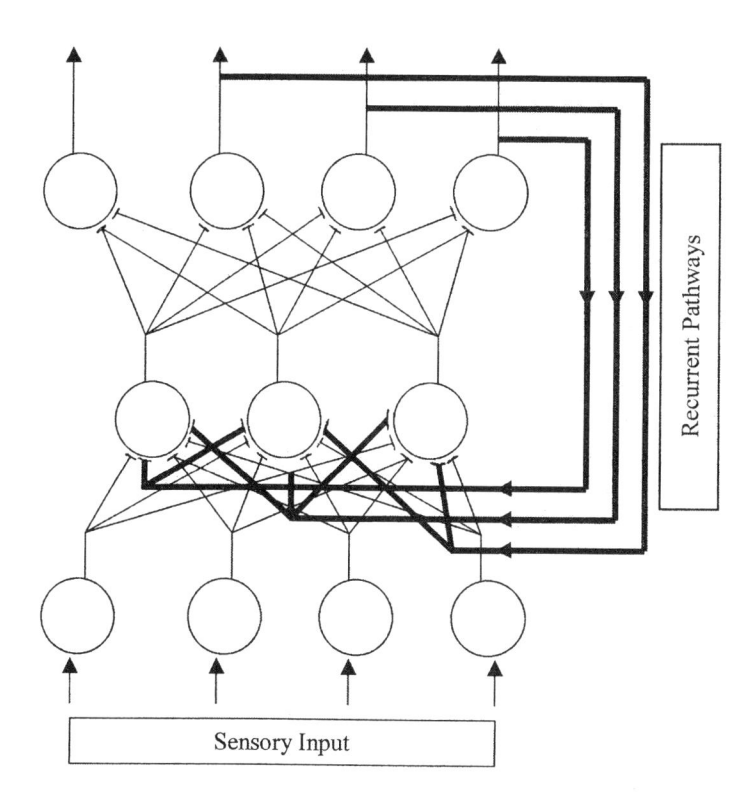

Figure 3.3: *Recurrent neural net.*[47] Large neural nets of this type have many of the properties which conscious states are thought to have.

One good way to test the ability of our conception of consciousness to undergo successful reduction is to make a list of the functions commonly attributed to consciousness, then see whether there is evidence that all of these functions are fulfilled by a single process. If the concept of consciousness is going to fragment, one would expect to find these functions achieved by different processes. If a single process can be found which achieves all of the important known functions of consciousness, hope can be held out for a non-eliminative reduction of consciousness. Paul Churchland provides a useful list of the primary functions of consciousness, and explains how a recurrent neural net might achieve them:

1. *Consciousness involves short-term memory.* The recurrent net in Figure 3.3 achieves something like this by way of its recurrent pathways, which are continuously active, preserving certain information while allowing other information to decay.

2. *Consciousness is independent of sensory inputs.* Consciousness continues in the absence of any input from the senses. One can still think, imagine, plan, remember, etc. without any sensory input at all—at least for a time, sensory deprivation experiments have shown that humans can only endure these states for limited periods. The brain needs to exercise itself, and in the absence of input, it will create its own "input," in much the same way that dreaming reveals the brain's insistence on keeping certain areas functioning in the absence of input. Recurrent nets also do not need input to run. The cycle running from the upper layer to the middle layer can still run in the absence of sensory input from the bottom layer.

3. *Consciousness displays steerable attention.* Paul Churchland describes how a recurrent net might be able to achieve an effect similar to the way that we can sensitize ourselves to certain sounds while ignoring others. A mother can hear her child above all sorts of background noises, for instance. A recurrent net can achieve something similar to this by putting itself into a state similar to the state it would go in if it actually received the target information.

There is a difference between this sort of priming effect and attention, however. I can prime myself to look for a certain thing, and then cease attending to that thing entirely. For instance, if I think a lot about Jaguars, I will still tend to notice Jaguars in traffic even when I am not currently thinking about them. The priming effect is still there without attention.

4. *Consciousness has the capacity for alternative explanations of complex or ambiguous data.* Certain visual illusions which can be seen two ways, such as the duck-rabbit, or the Necker cube illustrate this

phenomenon. Paul Churchland says that

> A recurrent network has the capacity, once more through its recurrent manipulation of its own cognitive processing, to bring different cognitive interpretations to bear on one and the same perceptual circumstance.[48]

5. *Consciousness disappears in deep sleep.* During slow wave sleep, which occurs several times during the night between stages of REM sleep, in which dreams are most likely to occur, consciousness disappears, even in its dreaming form. Consistent with Llinas' theory, it has been found that the activity of the intralaminar nuclei ceases during deep sleep.

6. *Consciousness reappears in dreaming*, at least in muted or disjointed form. Are dreams a form of conscious state? They share certain features, such as the coherent mixing of representations from the different modalities (see number 7, below; although taste and smell seem very weak or absent in dreams).

7. *Conscious states are blends of information from several different modalities.* Consciousness harbors the contents of the several basic sensory modalities within a single unified experience. Each of the senses responds to a range of properties of external objects: Vision responds to their light-reflective properties, hearing responds to any features of the object capable of generating sound waves, smell responds to certain types of molecules the object might give off, and so on. We know that information from each sensory modality is first processed separately. This unimodal information undergoes further processing, then mixes with information from other modalities, in what are known as multimodal areas. Paul Churchland argues that the intralaminar nuclei have the right sorts of connections to achieve a merging of this sort:

> Information from all of the sensory cortical areas is fed into the recurrent system, and it gets jointly and *collectively* represented in the coding vectors at the intralaminar nucleus, and in the axonal activity radiating outward from there.[49]

Again though, the brain goes through a lot of trouble to somehow merge the inputs from the different senses into a single conscious experience. Why does it do this?

Conclusion: The Imaginable and the Unimaginable

What is frustrating about the task of explaining consciousness is that it seems as if all the pieces of the puzzle are on the table in front of us. Surely the brain processes which are embodying conscious processes are large and have been detected by one of our dozens of techniques of monitoring the brain. We merely need to know which ones they are. Not so fast, say the holdouts. It is difficult (or impossible) for us to imagine how the brain can produce what we know as the mind. This may only indicate a limitation in our imaginations, the Churchlands would reply. But at other times, our imaginations are too powerful, in that they can represent events which are in fact impossible. In her article "Brainshy," Patricia Churchland has undertaken an examination of the role of the human imagination in the mind-brain debates.

The human mind has an intriguing susceptibility to certain types of ideas which seem clear to it, but do not represent anything in reality. And in some cases these ideas and thoughts *cannot* represent anything real, because it is impossible for what they describe to exist. Consider the idea of perpetual motion, something which still keeps stubborn tinkerers working long hours in their basements on "perpetual motion machines"—devices which operate without any energy input, sometimes by generating their own energy. But perpetual motion is impossible, because it violates laws of thermodynamics.[50]

Compare that with this proposal coming from the dualist camp: We seem to be able to imagine a being which is molecule-for-molecule identical to a given human, but which lacks consciousness.[51] Compare this in turn with the following case which shows clearly there is a problem: I can imagine something that is molecule-for-molecule the same as that magnet but which lacks the property of magnetism. I just imagine something that looks, feels, etc. just like that magnet but which does not attract iron filings or other magnetic metal. But this isn't enough; what I am trying to imagine contradicts laws of physics. The materialist argues similarly there simply cannot be a molecular duplicate which lacks consciousness.

At the other end, the fact that I *cannot* imagine something is simply "a (not very interesting) psychological fact about me," says Patricia Churchland,[52] and does not indicate that the unimaginable event is impossible. One thing which *is* of interest about such facts, however, is that they may contain important clues about how we represent events. Different types of representation systems have different limits on what they can represent. In learning that certain types of human cognition cannot represent something, we are learning about the nature of its primary representation system: the network of concepts. It is also worth noting that the limits of the imagination depends on the beliefs a person has; imagination occurs within the framework of a specific set of beliefs.

We are often fooled into thinking we can imagine how difficult a problem is before we find a solution to it. Hence Patricia Churchland criticizes David Chalmers' distinction between "easy problems," such as those involved in explaining perception and attention, and "the hard problem," of describing the ontological status of conscious states.[53]

> Before 1953, many people believed, on rather good grounds, actually, that in order to address the copying problem (transmission of traits from parents to offspring), you would first have to solve the problem of how proteins fold. The former was deemed to be a much harder problem than the latter, and many scientists believed it was foolhardy to attack the copying problem directly. As we all know now, the basic answer to the copying problem lay in the base-pairing of DNA, and it was solved first. Humbling it is to realize that the problem of protein folding (secondary and tertiary) is still not solved. That, given the lot we know now, does seem to be a hard problem.[54]

The only way to truly gauge a problem's degree of difficulty is to solve it. Using feelings of obviousness or of obtuseness to indicate a problem's level of difficulty is not a reliable technique. Of course, such feelings are useful on a rough-and-ready basis to guide one's thinking in the moment, but they cannot be the ultimate arbiters of a problem's difficulty level.

Imagination, in conclusion, is also one of the defining features of the Churchlands' work over the past twenty-five years. They were capable of imagining quite vividly a way in which folk psychology might disappear. Approaching the problem of consciousness also requires a limber yet accurate imagination. The Churchlands are always urging their readers to employ their imaginations in novel ways, especially when it comes to envisaging how neural activity can produce our mental lives. They have combined this productive power with an admirable ability to go into a new field and quickly master its important concepts and debates. Here it is difficult to exaggerate the magnitude of what they have accomplished. Contemporary science and philosophy on their own are difficult, but to formulate a consistent worldview which spans both requires a heroic mental effort. At least, for *one* person to achieve, but perhaps in the Churchlands' case, two brains together accomplished the task. Two brains who understand each other so well that the cognitive effort can be directed more at the problems themselves than at the difficulties of brain-to-brain communication.

Endnotes

[1] *Pacific Philosophical Quarterly* **64** (1983), 80-95.

[2] The phenomenon of hemineglect (see *Neurophilosophy*, 230-232), where right-hemisphere stroke seems to cause the left side of the body and its surrounding space to disappear from consciousness, is an example of a gap in consciousness.

[3] "Filling In: Why Dennett is Wrong," with V. S. Ramachandran. In *Dennett and His Critics,* ed. B. Dahlbom. Oxford: Blackwell, 1994.

[4] Those who prefer to use their right eyes can turn the diagram upside-down.

[5] Figure based on Fig. 8 from "Filling In: Why Dennett is Wrong," *Ibid*.

[6] M. Fiorini, M.G.P. Rosa, R. Gattass and C.E. Rocha-Miranda, "Dynamic Surrounds of Receptive Fields in Primate Striate Cortex: A Physiological Basis," *Proceedings of the National Academy of Science* **89** (1992), 8547-8551.

[7] For a review of recent work on filling in, see L. Pessoa, E. Thompson, and A. Noë, "Finding Out About Filling in: A Guide to Perceptual Completion for Visual Science and the Philosophy of Perception," *The Behavioral and Brain Sciences* **21**(6) (1998), 723-802.

[8] See Hilary Putnam's article "Minds and Machines," in *Dimensions of Mind*, ed. Sidney Hook, New York: New York University Press, 1960.

[9] See his book, *What Computers Can't Do*, Cambridge, Mass.: The MIT Press, 1972.

[10] See "Minds, Brains, and Programs," *The Behavioral and Brain Sciences* **3** (1980), 417-457.

[11] "Could a Machine Think?," *Scientific American* **262(1)** (1990), 32-37.

[12] *Ibid.*, 62.

[13] *Ibid.*, 55

[14] *Ibid.*, 50.

[15] *The Engine of Reason, the Seat of the Soul: A Philosophical Journey into the Brain,* Cambridge, Mass.: The MIT Press, 1995, 203.

[16] *The Rediscovery of the Mind*, Cambridge, Mass.: The MIT Press, 1992, 14.

[17] *The Engine of Reason, the Seat of the Soul*, 205.

[18] *The Rediscovery of the Mind*, 145.

[19] *The Rediscovery of the Mind*, Cambridge, Mass.: The MIT Press, 1994, 97.

[20] *The Rediscovery of the Mind*, 144.

[21] See "Recent Work on Consciousness: Philosophical, Empirical and Theoretical," *Seminars in Neurology* **17** (1997), 101-108.

[22] *Seminars in Neurology* **17,** 101-108, also reprinted as Chapter 11 of *On the Contrary: Critical Essays 1987-1997* (1998) Cambridge, Mass.: The MIT Press.

[23] From the 1998 version, 161.

[24] *Ibid.*, 161-162.

[25] *Ibid.* 163.

[26] One is also then obliged to explain how such a view avoids the homunculus fallacy, or simply avoids the obvious fallacy of treating consciousness as if it were a type of perception, a view widely rejected. I attempt this in Chap. 3 of *On Searle*, Belmont, Calif.: Wadsworth Publishers, 2001.

[27] "What Mary Didn't Know," *Journal of Philosophy* **83** (1986), 291-295.

[28] From *Neurophilosophy*, by Patricia Churchland, Cambridge, Mass.: The MIT Press, 1986, 331.

[29] In *The Philosophical Review* **83** (1974), 435-450.

[30] Leibniz' Law is: x and y are identical if and only if x and y share all their properties. The exact formulation of the law is somewhat controversial, but the arguments here are relying on what is considered to be the stronger half of the law, known as the *indiscernibility of identicals*: If x is identical to y, then x and y share all their properties.

[31] *Neurophilosophy*, 329.

[32] *Neurophilosophy*, 330, italics in the original.

[33] *The Engine of Reason, the Seat of the Soul*, 198.

[34] *Ibid.*, 199.

[35] *Ibid.*

[36] John Perry, "Self-Notions," *Logos* **11** (1990), 17-31.

[37] See "The Perception of Phantom Limbs," V.S. Ramachandran and William Hirstein, *Brain* **121** (1998), 1603-1630.

[38] See "Discriminating the Origin of Information," by Marcia K. Johnson for a review of the experimental literature on this phenomenon, which dates to 1910. In *Delusional Beliefs*, eds. T.F. Oltmanns and B.A. Maher, New York: John Wiley and Sons, 1988.

[39] See *The Emperor's New Mind*, by Roger Penrose, Oxford: Oxford Univ. Press, 1989; and "Quantum Coherence in Microtubules: A Neural Basis for Emergent Consciousness?," Stuart Hameroff, in the *Journal of Consciousness Studies* **1** (1994), 98-118.

[40] See Patricia Churchland's paper, "Brainshy: Nonneural Theories of Conscious Experience," (1998) in *Toward a Science of Consciousness 1996—The Second Tucson Discussions and Debates*, eds. S. Hameroff, A. Kaszniak, A. Scott, Cambridge, Mass.: The MIT Press.

[41] *On the Contrary: Critical Essays 1987-1997,* Cambridge, Mass.: The MIT Press, 1998, 229.

[42] "Brainshy," 120.

[43] "Gaps in Penrose's Toilings," Rick Grush and Patricia Churchland, in *On the Contrary: Critical Essays 1987-1997,* Cambridge, Mass.: The MIT Press, 1998.

[44] "Gaps in Penrose's Toilings," 225.

[45] *Thalamic Oscillations and Signalling,* eds. Rodolfo Llinas, Mircea Steriade, and Edward G. Jones, New York: Wiley, 1990.

[46] *The Engine of Reason, the Seat of the Soul,* 219.

[47] Figure based on Fig. 8.6 of Paul Churchland's, *The Engine of Reason, the Seat of the Soul,* Cambridge, Mass.: The MIT Press, 1995.

[48] *The Engine of Reason, the Seat of the Soul,* 218.

[49] *Ibid.,* 222.

[50] Alleged perpetual motion machines which produce more energy in the form of work than is input to them in the form of heat would violate the first law of thermodynamics ("conservation of energy"); those which can continuously perform work without a flow of heat from a warmer body to a cooler body violate the second law of thermodynamics ("entropy").

[51] See David Chalmers' book *The Conscious Mind: In Search of a Fundamental Theory,* Oxford: Oxford Univ. Press, 1996.

[52] "Brainshy," 115.

[53] See Chalmers' *The Conscious Mind.*

[54] "Brainshy," p. 116.

Bibliography

Selected Works

Books by Patricia Churchland

Neurophilosophy: Toward a Unified Science of the Mind-Brain (1986) Cambridge, Mass.: The MIT Press.

The Computational Brain (1992) P. S. Churchland and T.J. Sejnowski. Cambridge, Mass.: The MIT Press.

Neurophilosophy and Alzheimer's Disease (1992) Edited by Y. Christen and P. S. Churchland. Berlin: Spinger-Verlag.

The Mind-Brain Continuum (1996) Edited by R. R. Llinas and P. S. Churchland. Cambridge, Mass.: The MIT Press.

Books by Paul Churchland

Scientific Realism and the Plasticity of Mind (1979) Cambridge: Cambridge University Press.

Matter and Consciousness (1984) Cambridge, Mass.: The MIT Press.

Images of Science: Scientific Realism versus Constructive Empiricism, (1985) Chicago: University of Chicago Press.

A Neurocomputational Perspective: The Nature of Mind and the Structure of Science (1989) Cambridge, Mass.: The MIT Press.

The Engine of Reason, the Seat of the Soul: A Philosophical Journey into the Brain (1995) Cambridge, Mass.: MIT Press.

Articles by Patricia Churchland

"Fodor on Language Learning" (1978) *Synthese* **38**, 149-159.

"A Perspective on Mind-Brain Research" (1980) *The Journal of Philosophy* **77**, 185-207.

"Is Determinism Self-Refuting?" (1981) *Mind* **90**, 99-101.

"On the Alleged Backwards Referral of Experiences and its Relevance to the Mind-Body Problem" (1981) *Philosophy of Science* **48**, 165-181.

"Mind-Brain Reduction: New Light From the Philosophy of Science" (1982) *Neuroscience* **7**, 1041-1047.

"Consciousness: The Transmutation of a Concept" (1983) *Pacific Philosophical Quarterly* **64**, 80-95.

"Psychology and the Study of the Mind-Brain: Reply to Carr, Brown, and Sudevan" (1984) *Neuroscience* **13**, 1401-1404.

"Epistemology in the Age of Neuroscience" (1987) *The Journal of Philosophy* **84**, 544-552.

"The Significance of Neuroscience for Philosophy" (1988) *Trends In Neurosciences* **11**, 304-307.

"Reductionism and the Neurobiological Basis of Consciousness" (1988) In *Consciousness and Contemporary Science*, eds. A.M. Marcel and E. Bisiach, Oxford: Oxford Univ. Press.

"Computational Neuroscience" (1988) With T.J. Sejnowski, and C. Koch. *Science* **241**, 1299-1306.

"Perspectives on Cognitive Neuroscience" (1988) With T. J. Sejnowski. *Science* **242**, 741-745.

"Neural Representation and Neural Computation" (1989) With T.J. Sejnowski. In *Biological Computation and Mental Representation,* ed. L. Nadel. Cambridge, Mass.: MIT Press, 15-48.

"Brain and Cognition" (1989) With T. J. Sejnowski. In *Foundations of Cognitive Science,* ed. M. Posner. Cambridge, Mass.: MIT Press.

"Is Neuroscience Relevant to Philosophy?" (1990) In *Canadian Philosophers,*ed. D. Copp. University of Toronto Press.

"Our Brains, Ourselves: Reflections on Neuroethical Questions" (1991) In *Bioscience and Society,* ed. D.J. Roy, B. E. Wynne, and R. W. Old. Wiley & Sons.

"Consciousness and the Neurosciences: Philosophical and Theoretical Issues" (1994) With I. Farber. In *The Cognitive Neurosciences,* ed. M. Gazzaniga. Cambridge, Mass.: The MIT Press, 1295-1308.

"Filling In: Why Dennett is Wrong" (1994) With V. S. Ramachandran. In *Dennett and His Critics,* ed. B. Dahlbom. Oxford: Blackwell.

Bibliography

"A Critique of Pure Vision" (1994) With V. S. Ramachandran, and T. J. Sejnowski. In *Large-scale Neuronal Theories of the Brain,* ed. C. Koch. Cambridge, Mass.: The MIT Press.

"Gaps in Penrose's Toiling" (1995) With Rick Grush. *Journal of Consciousness Studies* **2**, 10-29.

"Can Neurobiology Teach us Anything About Consciousness?" (1995) (Expanded version of 1993). In: *The Mind, The Brain, and Complex Adaptive Systems*, eds. H. J. Morowitz and J. L. Singer. Reading, Mass.: Addison-Wesley.

"Toward a Neurobiology of the Mind" (1996) In *The Mind-Brain Continuum*, eds. R.R. Llinas and P. S. Churchland. Cambridge, Mass.: The MIT Press, 281-303.

"The Hornswoggle Problem" (1996) *Journal of Consciousness Studies* **3**, 402-408.

"Feeling Reasons" (1996) In *Decision-Making and the Brain,* eds. A. R. Damasio, H. Damasio, and Y. Christen. Berlin: Springer-Verlag, 181-199.

"Brainshy: Nonneural Theories of Conscious Experience" (1998). In: *Consciousness—Papers for Tucson II*. Editors Stuart Hameroff, Alfred Kaszniak, Alwyn Scott. Cambridge, Mass.: The MIT Press.

"Computation and the Brain" (1998) With Rick Grush. In *The MIT Encyclopedia of Cognitive Science*, ed. R. Wilson, Cambridge, Mass.: The MIT Press.

"What Can We Expect From a Theory of Consciousness?" (1998) In *Advances in neurology, Volume 77. Consciousness: At the Frontiers of Neuroscience,* eds. H. Jasper, L. Descarries, V. Castellucci, and S. Rossignol. Philadeplphia: Lippincott-Raven, 19-32.

Articles by Paul Churchland

"The Logical Character of Action Explanations" (1970) *The Philosophical Review* **79**(2), 214-236.

"Two Grades of Evidential Bias" (1975) *Philosophy of Science*, **42** (3), 250-259.

"Eliminative Materialism and the Propositional Attitudes" (1981) *Journal of Philosophy* **78**(2), 67-90.

Bibliography

"The Anti-Realist Epistemology of van Fraassen's *The Scientific Image*" (1982) *Pacific Philosophical Quarterly* **63**, 226-235.

"Is *Thinker* a Natural Kind?" (1982) *Dialogue* **21**(2), 223-238.

"The Ontological Status of Observables: In Praise of the Superempirical Virtues" (1985) In *Images of Science*, eds. P.M. Churchland, and C.A. Hooker. Chicago: University of Chicago Press, 35-47.

"Reduction, Qualia, and the Direct Introspection of Brain States" (1985) *Journal of Philosophy* **82**(1), 8-28.

"Some Reductive Strategies in Cognitive Neurobiology" (1986) *Mind* **95**, 279-309.

"The Continuity of Philosophy and the Sciences" (1986) *Mind and Language* **1**(1), 5-14.

"Cognitive Neurobiology: A Computational Hypothesis for Laminar Cortex" (1986) *Biology and Philosophy* **1**(1), 25-51

"Folk Psychology and the Explanation of Human Behavior" (1988) *Proceedings of the Aristotelian Society* (supplement) **62**, 209-221.

"Perceptual Plasticity and Theoretical Neutrality: A Reply to Jerry Fodor" (1988) *Philosophy of Science* **55** (2), 167-187.

"On the Nature of Theories: A Neurocomputational Perspective" (1989) In *The Nature of Theories*, Minnesota Studies in the Philosophy of Science, Volume 14, ed. C. W. Savage. Minneapolis: University of Minnesota Press.

"Activation Vectors Versus Propositional Attitudes: How the *Brain* Represents Reality" (1992) *Philosophy and Phenomenological Research* **52**, 419-424.

"State-Space Semantics and Meaning Holism" (1993) *Philosophy and Phenomenological Research* **53**, 667-672.

"The Neural Representation of Social Reality," (1994) in *Mind and Morals,* eds. L. May, M. Friedman, and A. Clark, Cambridge, Mass.: The MIT press.

"A Feedforward Network for Fast Stereo Vision With Movable Vision Plane," (1994) in *Android Epistemology: Human and Machine Cognition,* eds. K. Ford and P. Hayes. AAAI Press/The MIT Press.

"The Rediscovery of Light" (1996) *Journal of Philosophy* **93** (5), 211-228.

"Conceptual Similarity Across Sensory and Neural Diversity: The Fodor/Lepore Challenge Answered" (1998) *Journal of Philosophy*, **95**(1), 5-32.

Works by Paul and Patricia Churchland

"Functionalism, Qualia, and Intentionality" (1981) *Philosophical Topics* **1**, 121-145.

"Stalking the Wild Epistemic Engine" (1983) *Nous*, **17**, 5-18. (Symposium for the American Philosophical Association, Western Division, Chicago, March 1983.)

"Could a Machine Think? Recent Arguments and New Prospects" (1990) *Scientific American* **262**(1), 32-37. Reprinted in *Thinking Computers and Virtual Persons,* ed. E. Dietrich, Academic Press.

"Intertheoretic Reduction: A Neuroscientist's Field Guide" (1991) *Seminars in the Neurosciences* **2**: 249 - 256. Reprinted in: *Nature's Imagination,* ed. John Cornwell. Oxford: Oxford University Press, and in *The Mind-Body Problem: A Guide to the Current Debate,* eds.R. Warner and T Szubka. Oxford: Blackwell, 41-54.

Replies in *The Churchlands and Their Critics* (1996) ed. R. McCauley, Oxford: Blackwell.

"Recent Work on Consciousness: Philosophical, Empirical and Theoretical" (1997) *Seminars in Neurology* **17**, 101-108.

On the Contrary: Critical Essays 1987-1997 (1998) Cambridge, Mass.: The MIT Press.